Arthur
and the Lost Diary

ISBN 979-11-86701-05-8 14740

Longtail Books

Arthur
and the Lost Diary

For Laurie

Chapter 1

It was a busy afternoon at the library. Lots of people were **wander**ing about, choosing books or doing **research**.

At one table, Sue Ellen was sitting alone. She didn't look up when anyone walked by, nor did she pay any **attention** to passing **conversation**s. She was **concentrating** on writing in her diary.

Dear Diary: The library is a **crowd**ed place today. A lot of my friends are here **working on** school **project**s. Sometimes I think it's funny that I have so many different kinds of friends. I **wonder** sometimes why I'm friends with them and not with other people.

If I could make up some new friends, what kind would I want? Should they be friends who always give me presents or **volunteer** to clean up my room? Or maybe I'd like famous friends who **star** in TV shows or movies. What makes someone a real friend, anyway?

Sue Ellen put down her pen. That was enough for now. She loved having a diary, a special place to write down her **private** thoughts. It wasn't that her ideas were always great or important. But she liked putting the words on paper, where she could look at them.

She closed the diary and **trace**d the **edge** of the **binding** with her finger. Sue Ellen had **design**ed the **cover** herself. My Diary, she had **print**ed **neat**ly with a **sparkle** pen. Underneath, she had added PRIVATE and DO NOT OPEN in large **letter**s.

The library clock **struck** four times, **remind**ing Sue Ellen that it was time to go. She picked up all the books she wanted to **check out** and **pile**d them on her school notebook and diary. She **tuck**ed everything underneath her arm as she walked to the **circulation** desk. She had to **shift** her arm to stay **balance**d, and when she did, her diary **slip**ped out of the pile and fell silently onto the carpet.

Ms. Turner sat at the checkout **counter**, waiting to help people with their books. She smiled when she saw Sue Ellen.

"That's an **impress**ive pile. I see you're going to be reading a lot this week."

"I couldn't **make up my mind**," Sue Ellen **admit**ted. "There were so many good books to choose from."

As Ms. Turner began checking out the books, Sue Ellen **spread** them on the counter.

When she got to the last one, she **expect**ed to see her diary underneath.

But all she saw was her notebook.

Immediately, she **search**ed among the other books.

"Is anything wrong?" asked Ms. Turner.

"No, I don't think . . . Well, yes." Sue Ellen looked around the floor. All she saw were two paper **clip**s and a pencil **erase**r.

"I think I lost something!" she said.

Quickly, she **retrace**d her **step**s to the table where she had been sitting. The diary wasn't there. Where could it have gone? Diaries don't **disappear** like magic. And they don't walk away by themselves.

She **knelt** down and searched under the chairs and tables, pushing aside feet when she had to.

"Excuse me. **Ouch!** Watch my fingers. Coming through."

Sue Ellen searched everywhere she could

My Diary
Private
Do Not Open

remember walking—and also a few places she hadn't. She even looked through the **waste**baskets.

But it was no good. The diary was nowhere to be found.

Sue Ellen **drag**ged herself back to the **checkout counter**. Her face was red, and her eyes **watery**.

"What's wrong?" asked Ms. Turner, who could see that Sue Ellen was upset.

"I lost my diary. I had it a minute ago. I don't understand. I must have left it here." She **scan**ned the counter again. "But I guess I didn't."

"Books don't get lost in my library," Ms. Turner **assure**d her. "**Describe** it to me."

Sue Ellen took a deep **breath**. "Well, it kind of looks like a book. It has a **shiny** red **leather cover**. Well, at least it looks like leather. And there are some blue **sparkle letter**s that say My Diary. And under that I wrote PRIVATE. DO NOT OPEN."

"That's very **specific**," said Ms. Turner. "It should make our **search** easier. Don't worry—we'll find it. I'll tell everyone on the **staff** to **be on the lookout**."

"Thanks. I guess I'll keep looking myself. I just wish . . ."

Sue Ellen **pause**d because she heard some laughing. It was **exact**ly the kind of sound a girl might make if she was looking at a secret diary.

"I'll be back," she told Ms. Turner.

Sue Ellen **trace**d the sound to the corner, where Francine was **hunch**ed over some pages.

"So that's where it went!" said Sue Ellen.

She **march**ed up to the desk.

"Pretty funny, huh, Francine?"

Francine **nod**ded. "I'll say. Listen to this—"

"I don't have to listen to it," said Sue Ellen. "I wrote it!" She **snatch**ed the book away from Francine.

"Hey!"

"And there's nothing funny about **steal**ing someone's diary. I'm surprised at you, Francine. I thought you were my—" Sue Ellen looked down at the book. It was red, but it didn't have blue sparkle letters. "Hey, this isn't my diary."

"Of course not," said Francine. "It's a **joke** book. What would I be doing with your diary?"

"I don't know. You could have picked it up. It's red and says PRIVATE on it. I had it a minute ago, and now it's gone."

"How **mysterious**," said Francine. "Do you think it was stolen?"

Sue Ellen didn't know what to think. "It was only **valuable** to me. I've been writing in it forever."

"I've never had a diary," said Francine. "What do you write in it?"

"My ideas, what's happened during the day. Private thoughts. It's very important that I find it, Francine. I mean, there's **stuff** in there about everyone."

Francine's eyes opened wide. "Everyone? When you say *everyone*, you mean *everyone?*"

"Yes, yes, but that's not what **matter**s now."

"It matters to me," said Francine. "What have you been writing?"

"I can't talk about that now. I have to find my diary."

Before Francine could say anything more, Sue Ellen **rush**ed off. If she didn't find the diary soon, she didn't know what she would do.

ELIZA

Chapter 3

"What's wrong with Sue Ellen?" Muffy asked Francine.

"She's all upset about losing her diary. It says PRIVATE on the front of it. She even thought I was reading it." Francine shook her head. "I don't see why that would upset her."

"Hmmm," said Muffy. "Maybe she wrote something in it about you—something she doesn't want you to read."

"About me?" Francine put her hands on her **hip**s. "But what would she write about me?"

"Maybe all the **mean** things you've done

to her."

Francine looked surprised. "What things?"

Muffy **fold**ed her arms. "Like pushing her in the **mud** yesterday."

"I did not push her," Francine **insist**ed. "She **trip**ped."

"Right next to you, though."

"I just happened to be there. I don't push people in the mud."

"Well, you laughed."

"Of course, I laughed. It was funny. She was covered with mud."

Muffy **cross**ed her arms. "You were standing next to her when she fell, and you laughed **afterward**. What if she *thinks* you pushed her?"

Francine **bit** her lip.

*She suddenly saw a **beard**ed doctor in a white coat sitting behind a large desk. After a **knock** at the door, Sue Ellen came in. She was **spatter**ed in mud.*

*"Do you have an **appointment**?" asked the doctor.

"No," Sue Ellen **admit**ted, "but I have to see you **at once**, Dr. Zimmer. It's an **emergency**."

"Ah! And what is the **nature** of this emergency?

Sue Ellen held out her arms. "Can't you tell? Francine just pushed me in the mud."

The doctor **stroke**d his beard. "So I see," he said.

Sue Ellen **consult**ed her diary. "That's the seventeenth time this month that Francine has been mean to me. Something must be done! I came to you because you're the world's **lead**ing **specialist** in mean children."

"True, true," said the doctor. "May I see that?" He took the diary from Sue Ellen and looked through it quickly.

"Ah, yes," he said. "Pushing. Laughing. Eating the fruit **filling** in your **snack** pie and leaving you only the **crust**." He **sigh**ed. "I'm **afraid** your friend **exhibit**s all the **sign**s of **acute** ogre-ism.*"

"Ogre-ism?"

*"**Exact**ly." The doctor pushed a button on his desk, and a **flicker**ing TV screen **appear**ed on the wall. It showed a girl screaming at other children. Then she pushed one of them down.*

*"As you can see," the doctor continued, "this is a **disease** in which the **victim** cannot control her meanness."*

"That's Francine!"

Dr. Zimmer stopped the film. "We have been watching her for a long time. I'm afraid there's no help for her. We must keep her away from the other children!"

*At that moment Francine **burst** in on them. She **point**ed a finger at Sue Ellen. "I thought I'd find you here!"*

*But before Francine could do anything **further**, two **uniform**ed **guard**s ran in and **restrain**ed her.*

★ **ogre-ism** 오거(Ogre)는 중세 기사 이야기에 등장하는 거인을 말한다. 여기에서는 -ism을 붙여 '아주 못된 행동을 하는 병'이라는 의미로 쓰였다.

"Leave me alone!" Francine shouted.

*"Sorry," said one of the guards, "but ogre-ism is very **contagious**. We must **remove** you at once."*

*"**Besides**," said the second guard, "the other children don't want to play with you. You've been too mean to them."*

"But I can change! Really!"

The guards laughed.

"If we had a nickel★ for every time we heard that one . . . ," said the first guard.

"We would have a lot of nickels," the second guard finished up.

Then they both laughed again.

★ **nickel** 미국이나 캐나다에서 쓰이는 5센트 동전.

Chapter 4

"But you have to give me another chance," said Francine. "I don't have ogre-ism."

"You don't have what?" Muffy asked.

Francine **blink**ed. She was back in the library.

"It's a **disease**. Sue Ellen may have written about it in her diary."

Francine stood up and **wipe**d her **forehead**. "I need a drink."

She **head**ed off for the water **fountain**.

"Francine is so **excitable** sometimes," Muffy said to herself. "Sue Ellen probably didn't write about her at all." She **pause**d, **lean**ing against a

shelf. "Of course, she did have to write about something. Everyday events can be so **boring,** though. She probably has to **make up** stories. . . ."

*Muffy saw herself looking into a long mirror. She was dressed as a princess, in a long **flowing** dress with a **jewel**ed **crown** on her head.*

*Sue Ellen was standing next to her. She was wearing a **plain** dress with no **jewelry**.*

*"Princess Millicenta," said Sue Ellen, "there is no one who **compares** with you."*

*"**Go on**," said Muffy.*

"You are rich."

"True."

"You are beautiful"

"True again."

"And you are the smartest princess in the land."

"Three for three," Muffy agreed.

*"You are so **fair**," Sue Ellen went on, "while I am just okay."*

*A shadow **hid** the sun for a moment.*

*"Who **dares** to **interrupt** my fine weather?" asked Muffy.*

*Sue Ellen looked out the window and **gasp**ed. "It's a dragon!" she cried. "A fire-**breathing** dragon. And it's causing big trouble in the **village**."*

*Muffy **comb**ed her hair. "What are the villagers doing about it?"*

"They're running this way!"

*"They are?" The princess was **alarm**ed.*

"Help us!" shouted the villagers. "Help us, rich and beautiful and smart Princess Millicenta!"

*Muffy **sigh**ed. "I guess we should do something."*

*"Fear not, princess!" said Sue Ellen, putting on a **suit** of **armor**. "I'll **handle** this!"*

*She started **clank**ing down the tower stairs, but after a few moments, the clanking stopped.*

*"What's the **matter**?" asked Muffy. "Why have you stopped?"*

*"Ooof," Sue Ellen called up. "I'm **stuck** in the*

doorway." She gasped. *"And the dragon is approaching!"*

Muffy looked out the window. The dragon was on its way up the hill.

Muffy sighed. "If you want something done right, you've got to do it yourself."

She took the end of her long, **braid**ed hair and **thread**ed it through a **handy pulley** outside the window. Then she lowered herself to the ground.

As the dragon **prepare**d to **toast** Sue Ellen to a **crisp**, Muffy **spritz**ed it with a bottle of her **perfume**.

The dragon's fire was **snuff**ed out.

"Oh, princess!" **gush**ed Sue Ellen. "My thanks! I don't know how I can ever **repay** you!"

"Well, this perfume is thirty dollars a bottle. You can start there."

Sue Ellen sighed. "You must be the most **practical** princess in the world."

"Yes," Muffy said happily. "I **suppose** I am."

"Hey, space cadet!★" said Binky, **tap**ping Muffy on the shoulder.

Muffy **blink**ed. "What's that? You can't talk to me that way. I'm a princess."

Binky just **shrug**ged. "Okay, okay. But whatever you are, you're **block**ing the **shelf**. I need to look for a book back there."

"Oh, sorry." Muffy **step**ped **aside**. "I guess I was thinking about Sue Ellen's diary. She lost it."

★ **space cadet** 멍한 사람 또는 현실과 동떨어진 사람을 가리키는 표현.

"**Tough** luck."

"It had the most wonderful story about me. . . ."

Binky looked **confuse**d. "I thought this was Sue Ellen's diary."

"Well, it is. But a diary is a good place to write about your friends."

"Really?" said Binky. "What did this diary look like?"

"I'm not sure. But it said PRIVATE on it."

"I saw a book like that," said Binky. "It was on the floor. I put it on one of the **cart**s."

"You did?"

Binky **nod**ded. "It's not good to leave books on the floor."

"Did you look inside it?" Muffy asked.

"No," said Binky. "Why would I? The report I'm doing isn't on anything PRIVATE."

"I know, I know," said Muffy. "But that's not the **point**. A diary can be very, um, interesting. People write down how they really feel about everything."

"*Everything?*"

Muffy nodded. "And everybody. I just hope we can find it."

She left to see if she could help with the **search**.

Binky was **impress**ed. "Everybody, huh?" he said to himself. Keeping a diary sounded like a lot of work. Writing one didn't **appeal** to him. But if Sue Ellen was writing about everybody . . .

Binky **reach**ed up to get a book, but his arm **froze** in **midair**.

"That would even **include** me!" he **realize**d.

Binky saw Sue Ellen sitting at a desk in her bedroom. She was writing in her diary.

Dear Diary: Today was very special. I was able to spend almost all my time with Binky Banes, the man of my dreams.

*She **drew** a picture of Binky in the **margin**. He had on sunglasses like a movie star.*

He's so handsome—and strong, too. Today the school bus got **stuck** in the **mud**, and Binky **volunteered** to go **lift** up the back end. The bus driver said that wouldn't be **necessary**. But Binky did it anyway, and the driver didn't seem to **mind**.

I can tell that the other boys all **look up to** Binky. Who can **blame** them? I only wish I could get Binky to **notice** me. I try smiling at him a lot, but he only asks me what's wrong with my face. I follow him around on the **playground**, but he wants to know if I'm lost or something. I've even started bringing him extra **dessert**s for lunch. At least that gets his **attention**. And I know he likes the desserts because he always **burps afterward**.

I'm not sure I can **go on**, though, without letting him know how I feel. Maybe tonight I should go over to his house and **serenade** him under his window. If that doesn't show him, nothing will.

34

"What's the **matter**, Binky?" said Arthur. "You look like the Statue of Liberty.★"

"Huh?" Binky **drop**ped his arm like a stone.

Arthur was **load**ed down with the **stack** of books he had picked out. "Are you all right? You look a little **strange**."

"No, no, I'm fine. Don't forget, I can **lift** the back of a bus."

"You can what?"

"Um, **never mind**." Binky wanted to change

★ **Statue of Liberty** 자유의 여신상. 미국 뉴욕항의 리버티섬에 있는 여신상을 가리킨다.

the **subject**. "Did you hear? Sue Ellen lost her diary. I put it on the **cart**."

Arthur **frown**ed. "Why didn't you give it back to her?"

"I didn't know it was her diary then. It was just some book with PRIVATE written across the front."

"PRIVATE?" said Arthur. "I **wonder** why."

Binky **shudder**ed. "You can wonder all you want, but don't **expect** any help from me. I'm done wondering. See you later."

"Bye," said Arthur. He thought Binky was acting a little **odd**. Maybe holding his arm up like that had **cut off** the blood **supply** to his brain.

It was too bad about Sue Ellen's diary. Arthur knew that people didn't always say everything they were thinking in **public**. But in her diary, especially with all that PRIVATE **stuff**, Sue Ellen probably didn't **hold back**.

"Arthur, what are you doing with all those books?"

"Doing?" said Arthur. "I'm planning to take them out."

Sue Ellen looked at the titles. "**Mystery** of the **Mummy**'s **Curse, Eerie Canal**s of Mars.* Arthur, I can't believe you read this stuff."

"Why not?"

"It's not good for you. Don't you get **nightmare**s?"

"Not from reading," said Arthur "I like **adventure**s."

"Oh, really? Have you had any nightmares in the last week?"

"I—I guess so."

Sue Ellen **fold**ed her arms. "And have you read any of these kinds of books in the last week?"

"Well, yes . . ."

★**Mars** 화성. 지구의 밖을 돌고 있는 첫 번째의 외행성이며, 태양을 중심으로 4번째 궤도를 공전하는 태양계 행성이다.

"I rest my case,★" said Sue Ellen. *"You know, Arthur, I've been watching you very closely."*

"You have?"

Sue Ellen nodded. "You're not perfect, Arthur. **In fact***, you're wide open for* **improve***ment I've* **kept track of** *your* **flaw***s in my diary."*

"You shouldn't have gone to all that trouble," *said Arthur.*

"Oh, it's no trouble," said Sue Ellen. "I keep everything **organize***d in my diary. But I can't just write about these things anymore. I have to* **take action***."*

"What kind of action?"

"To **shape** *you people* **up***. I've made a list of the ways you could change."*

She took a **scroll** *of paper out of her pocket. It* **unroll***ed down to her feet and* **halfway** *across the room.*

★**I rest my case** '자, 내가 말한 대로잖아'라는 뜻의 표현. 주로 법정에서 변호사가 자신의 논지를 충분히 입증했다는 의미로 쓰인다.

Arthur
FLAWS

"'Number 1,'" she read aloud.

Arthur **sigh**ed. He looked around for a way to escape.

Sue Ellen stopped reading. "I know that look. Maybe we should **skip direct**ly to Number 78."

Arthur was almost **afraid** to ask. "What's that?" he said finally.

Sue Ellen moved along the paper. "'Number 78: Doesn't take **criticism** well.' Now, are you going to sit still? We've got work to do."

There didn't seem to be any way out. But as Sue Ellen went **hunt**ing for the top of the list, she moved **slight**ly to one side. Arthur saw his chance—and **dove** through an opening in the book**shelves**.

Chapter 7

"Hey! **Watch out!**" cried one of the library **assistant**s as Arthur **crash**ed into his cart.

The books went flying.

"Sorry," said Arthur, **pick**ing **himself up** off the floor. "I was trying to . . . Well, **never mind**."

"Look at this **mess**," said the assistant. He started picking the books up.

"Here, let me help," said Arthur.

The assistant jumped back. "How do I know you won't try to **tackle** me again?"

"I wasn't tackling you," said Arthur. "I was

just trying to escape."

"Escape? Escape from what?"

Arthur **shrug**ged. "It's not important. I'm safe now. So please let me help."

"Okay. But just remember, I've **got my eye on** you."

Arthur began **gather**ing some of the books. They came in all different sizes and **subject**s. One, in **particular**, caught his **attention**. It said PRIVATE on the front.

At the other end of the library, Binky, Muffy, and Francine were **hunt**ing as a team. The girls were looking through the **bookcase**s, checking on the desks and chairs.

Binky was down **on his hands and knees.**

"Here, little diary," he said. "Come out, come out, wherever you are."

Francine **gave** him **a look**. "Do you really think that will help?"

"It can't hurt," Binky **insist**ed.

"The diary shouldn't be that hard to find," said Muffy.

Francine **frown**ed. "**Unless** somebody else has found it first."

Muffy **gasp**ed.

"What's wrong?" Binky and Francine asked together.

"Nothing," said Muffy. "I was just thinking. What if a **big-time** movie **producer** found the diary? She might want to make a movie about it. The movie would be a giant success. Everyone in it would be known all over the world. Wouldn't that be great?"

Francine and Binky **stare**d at each other. "No!" they shouted.

"Look harder," said Francine.

"Much harder," Binky added.

They **renew**ed the **search** as Arthur **came by**.

"Muffy, have you—"

"No questions now, Arthur. Can't you see I'm busy?"

Actually, Arthur had **wonder**ed why Muffy was looking under the seat **cushion**s. He had never seen her do that before.

"I just wanted to know if you've seen Sue Ellen."

"Not for a while."

"Can you—?"

"Do I need to **spell** it out for you, Arthur? I'm *B-U-S-Y.* **Get the message?**"

"**Loud and clear.**"

Arthur moved over to where Francine was **flip**ping **through** some newspapers.

"What about you, Francine?"

"What about me?"

"Have you seen Sue Ellen?"

"Arthur, I'm not **keep**ing **track of** anybody right now. I have a job to do."

"If you could just . . . Whoa! Binky, what are you doing?"

Binky had **lift**ed one of Arthur's feet into the air.

"Just checking," he said. He put Arthur's foot back down.

"Well, **leave** my feet **out of** it. **By the way**, you haven't seen Sue Ellen, have you?"

"I can't see anyone from down here," Binky **admit**ted.

Arthur **scratch**ed his head. "Why are you down there, anyway? Wait, don't tell me. I have to go find Sue Ellen."

"What's so important that you have to find her now?" Muffy asked.

"Oh, I found her diary."

Everyone **froze**.

Arthur, Muffy, Binky, and Francine sat around the table. Sue Ellen's diary sat in the middle. The word PRIVATE seemed to be **glaring** at them from the **cover**.

Binky **reach**ed for it, but Arthur put his hand on the cover.

"I really don't think we should do this," he said. "I mean, would you want someone to read *your* diary?"

"I don't *have* a diary," said Binky, "so how would *I* know?" Still, he **hesitate**d.

"**Honest**ly, Arthur," said Francine, "don't you

want to know what she wrote about you?"

"Well . . . kind of . . . I guess."

"It's **settle**d, then," said Muffy. "Who's going to read first?"

Francine and Binky looked at each other. "Not me," they said together.

"**Definite**ly not me," said Arthur.

"Well, I don't want to be first," said Muffy. "I know . . . We could **spin** the diary around like a **compass**. When it stopped, the top would **point** to one of us. That person would have to open it."

"Sounds **fair**," said Francine.

"Yes," agreed Binky.

"Very," said Arthur.

"So, should we spin?" asked Muffy.

"NOOOO!" everyone else shouted.

"Maybe we could just stand it on end," said Francine. "Maybe it would fall over and open."

"That would almost be an **accident**," said

Muffy. "I like it."

They placed the diary **upright**.

"It looks **wobbly**," said Francine.

"Wobbly is good," Binky agreed.

The diary may have looked wobbly, but it didn't move.

"Maybe we're not **staring** hard enough," said Muffy.

Francine **blink**ed. "I can't stare any harder. I'm getting **cross-eyed**."

"What if a strong wind came in and **knock**ed the diary open?" said Muffy.

"Yeah," said Francine. "And that same wind might **flip** the pages. . . ."

They waited **patient**ly for a wind to **come by**. They waited and waited.

"Muffy, what are you doing?" asked Arthur.

Muffy **blush**ed. "Me? Nothing."

"There! You did it again." Arthur pointed a finger at her. "You're **blow**ing at the book."

"Don't be **silly**," said Muffy. "I'm just, um, doing some **breathing exercise**s."

Binky **snort**ed. "Well, you're going to have to breathe a lot harder if you want to get anywhere."

He **let out** a very deep **breath**.

"And what was that?" asked Arthur.

"Just a **sigh**, Arthur," said Francine. "You can't **blame** Binky for sighing. I think a little sigh would do me some good."

Arthur **cross**ed his arms. "Now you're all **huff**ing **and puff**ing. It's not right."

"I have to agree with Arthur," said Binky. "I don't think the wind is going to be enough. What we need is an **earthquake**."

"Not much chance of that," said Arthur.

"You never know," said Binky, kicking the table hard.

The book fell over—but it was still shut.

"Hey!" said Arthur. "That's **cheat**ing."

"It was just an **experiment**," Binky **insist**ed.

TUCKER
My
Diary
Private
Do Not Open

"I wanted to see if an earthquake would help."

"Forget the wind and the earthquake," said Francine. "Maybe we should just all read it together. That way we'll all be **equa**lly . . . **guilty**."

Nobody could **argue** with that.

Chapter 9

"My whole life is in that diary!" said Sue Ellen.

"I'm sure it is," said Ms. Turner. She had taken Sue Ellen into the **staff** room to **console** her.

Sue Ellen **sigh**ed. "And now my whole life is gone."

"There, there, dear. You still have your life, **after all**. As for your diary, I'm sure it will **turn up**. Diaries don't just **vanish into thin air**."

"I've had that diary ever since I was six. I started it on the first day of first grade."

"Really," said Ms. Turner.

"That was my very first whole day of school.

I had never been in school that long before. When I got home, my mother helped me write down everything about it."

Ms. Turner **nod**ded.

"We started with Circle Time.★ I had a hard time sitting still. And I remember **staring** at another little girl because I had never seen anyone so **dress**ed **up**. Then the teacher read us a story. 'The Three Bears,✳' I think. I kept calling out for Goldilocks✳ to be careful, but I remember feeling sorry for the bears at the end. At least I think I did. I'd have to check in my—" Sue Ellen **bit** her lip. "But I can't check it, can I?"

Ms. Turner stood up and **rub**bed her hands

★ **Circle Time** 이야기 나누기 활동. 아이들이 둥그렇게 모여 앉아서 차례대로 이야기를 하거나 다같이 노래를 부르는 것을 말한다.

✳ **The Three Bears** '곰 세 마리 이야기'라는 영국의 전래동화. 골디락스라는 소녀가 어느 날 숲에서 길을 잃었다가 세 마리의 곰이 사는 오두막에 들어가면서 벌어지는 이야기를 담고 있다.

✳ **Goldilocks** 골디락스. '곰 세 마리 이야기'에 등장하는 소녀의 이름으로 'gold(금)'와 'lock(머리카락)' 두 단어가 합쳐진 말로 금발을 뜻한다.

together. "You know, maybe instead of sitting here, we'd **be better off** continuing the **hunt**."

"What if someone else finds it first?"

Ms. Turner **pat**ted Sue Ellen on the shoulder. "Then they'll **turn** it **in** at the desk, and all will be well."

Sue Ellen shook her head. "But what if that person reads the diary before returning it? No one **besides** me has ever read it."

"Now, Sue Ellen, I think you're getting yourself upset over nothing. You told me it says PRIVATE in big **letter**s right where everyone can see it."

"That's true," Sue Ellen **admit**ted.

"Why,* then, you have nothing to worry about."

"Sue Ellen!"

Arthur and the others were coming toward her.

★ **why** 이유를 묻거나 말할 때 쓰는 의문사 또는 관계사가 아닌 '그럼', '어머', 또는 '아니'라는 뜻의 감탄사로 쓰였다.

"We have something for you," said Arthur. He held out the diary.

Sue Ellen **gasp**ed. "Where did you find it?" She took the diary and **hug**ged it against her **chest**.

"On one of the **cart**s," said Arthur. "I was going to give it right back to you—"

"But we stopped him," said Muffy.

"Because we wanted to look inside," Francine added.

"You did?" Sue Ellen hugged the diary tighter. "But it's PRIVATE. It says so right on the **cover**."

"Don't worry," said Arthur. "We didn't look."

"Even though we were **tempt**ed by winds and **earthquake**s," said Binky.

Sue Ellen didn't understand, but she smiled anyway. "Well, whatever the reason, thank you. And even though I'm breaking one of my **rule**s, I can tell you what I'm going to write tonight."

"What's that?" asked Binky.

Sue Ellen smiled. "That I have the best friends in the world."

As Sue Ellen was leaving the library, Binky held open the door for her.

"**Allow me**," he said.

Sue Ellen looked surprised. "Why, Binky, I didn't know you were such a gentleman."

"I'm not! That is, well, not usually." He looked at the ground. "And if you tell anyone, I'll **deny** it."

Sue Ellen smiled. "Don't worry. Your secret is safe with me."

She continued on to the bike **rack**, where Muffy was just getting ready to leave.

"See you later, Sue Ellen." Muffy put her foot on the **pedal**—and then stopped. "**By the way**, I'll be home tonight if you need any ideas for stories."

"Stories?"

"You know, something about a beautiful, rich, and **resourceful** princess saving the world."

"Oh. Thank you, Muffy. If that **comes up**, I'll give you a call."

Muffy **nod**ded and **rode** off.

"Oh, Sue Ellen," said Francine, running up behind her, "let me hold your books while you un**lock** your bike. Wouldn't want you to get hurt!"

"Um, thanks."

"Is there anything else I can help you with? I'm very **friendly**, you know. And **considerate**, too. And have I **mention**ed *nice?* Being nice is my best thing."

Sue Ellen looked **confuse**d.

"Well, see you tomorrow," said Francine. "Call me if you have any problems with your homework or if you just want to talk. And happy writing!"

Sue Ellen shook her head as she put on her bike helmet. She would never have **expect**ed that writing a diary would make her so popular.

She was still thinking about this as Arthur came out of the library.

"Arthur, are you sure nobody read my diary?" she asked.

"Don't worry, Sue Ellen. It's still **private**." He **paused**. "Is there anything else you want to ask me? Or maybe tell me?"

"I don't think so."

"You know, I take **criticism** really well. And I'm always ready to **improve** myself. So don't **hold back**."

Sue Ellen got on her bike. "I won't. You're sure about the diary. . . ."

My Diary
Private
DO NOT OPEN

"**Positive.**"

"That's good. You might have been **embarrass**ed."

"Me?" Arthur **blink**ed. "I **suppose** you've written down a lot of ways I could improve."

Sue Ellen looked **puzzle**d. "No. Actually, I said some pretty nice things about you."

Arthur **blush**ed. "Really? Like what?"

"Sorry. My lips are **seal**ed."

Arthur **frown**ed. "That's not **fair!**"

"See you later!" said Sue Ellen, riding off.

"All right," Arthur called after her. "**In that case**, I'm going to start a diary of my own."

Sue Ellen **screech**ed to a stop.

"You are? What are you going to **put in** it?"

Arthur smiled. "That," he said, "will be my little secret."

아서와
사라진 일기장

아서와
사라진 일기장

CONTENTS

대한민국 영어 학습자라면 꼭 한번 읽어봐야 할, 아서 챕터북 시리즈!

아서 챕터북 시리즈(Arthur Chapter Book series)는 미국의 작가 마크 브라운(Marc Brown)이 쓴 책입니다. 레이크우드 초등학교에 다니는 주인공 아서(Arthur)가 소소한 일상에서 벌이는 다양한 에피소드를 담은 이 책은, 기본적으로 미국 초등학생들을 위해 쓰인 책이지만 누구나 공감할 만한 재미있는 스토리로 출간된 지 30년이 넘은 지금까지 남녀노소 모두에게 큰 사랑을 받고 있습니다. 아서가 주인공으로 등장하는 이야기는 리더스북과 챕터북 등 다양한 형태로 출판되었는데, 현재 미국에서만 누적 판매 부수가 6천6백만 부를 돌파한 상황으로 대한민국 인구 숫자보다 더 많은 책이 판매된 것을 생각하면 그 인기가 어느 정도 인지 실감할 수 있습니다.

특히 이『아서 챕터북』은 한국에서 영어 학습자를 위한 최적의 원서로 큰 사랑을 받고 있기도 합니다.『영어 낭독 훈련』,『잠수네 영어 학습법』,『솔빛이네 엄마표 영어연수』등 많은 영어 학습법 책들에서『아서 챕터북』을 추천 도서로 선정하고 있으며, 수많은 영어 고수들과 영어 선생님들, '엄마표 영어'를 진행하는 부모님들에게도 반드시 거쳐 가야 하는 영어원서로 전폭적인 지지를 얻고 있습니다.

번역과 단어장이 포함된 워크북, 그리고 오디오북까지 담긴 풀 패키지!

이 책은 이렇게 큰 사랑을 받고 있는 영어원서『아서 챕터북』시리즈에, 더욱 탁월한 학습 효과를 거둘 수 있도록 다양한 콘텐츠를 덧붙인 책입니다.

- 영어원서: 본문에 나온 어려운 어휘에 볼드 처리가 되어 있어 단어를 더욱 분명히 인지하며 자연스럽게 암기하게 됩니다.
- 단어장: 원서에 나온 어려운 어휘가 '한영'은 물론 '영영' 의미까지 완벽하게 정리되어 있으며, 반복되는 단어까지 넣어두어 자연스럽게 복습이 되도록 구성했습니다.
- 번역: 영어와 비교할 수 있도록 직역에 가까운 번역을 담았습니다. 원서 읽기에 익숙하지 않은 초보 학습자들도 어려움 없이 내용을 파악할 수 있습니다.
- 퀴즈: 현직 원어민 교사가 만든 이해력 점검 퀴즈가 들어있습니다.
- 오디오북: 미국 현지에서 판매중인 빠른 속도의 오디오북(분당 약 145단어)과

국내에서 녹음된 따라 읽기용 오디오북(분당 약 110단어)을 포함하고 있어 듣기 훈련은 물론 소리 내어 읽기에까지 폭넓게 사용할 수 있습니다.

- 미국 원어민 기준: 유치원 ~ 초등학교 저학년
- 한국 학습자 기준: 초등학교 저학년 ~ 중학교 1학년
- 영어원서 완독 경험이 없는 초보 영어 학습자 (토익 기준 450~750점대)
- 비슷한 수준의 다른 챕터북: Magic Tree House, Marvin Redpost, Zack Files, Captain Underpants
- 도서 분량: 5,000단어 초반 (약 5,000~5,200단어)

아서 챕터북, 이렇게 읽어보세요!

- **단어 암기는 이렇게!** 처음 리딩을 시작하기 전, 해당 챕터에 나오는 단어들을 눈으로 쭉 훑어봅니다. 모르는 단어는 좀 더 주의 깊게 보되, 손으로 써가면서 완벽하게 암기할 필요는 없습니다. 본문을 읽으면서 이 단어들을 다시 만나게 되는데, 그 과정에서 단어의 쓰임새와 어감을 자연스럽게 익히게 됩니다. 이렇게 책을 읽은 후에, 단어를 다시 한번 복습하세요. 복습할 때는 중요하다고 생각하는 단어들을 손으로 써가면서 꼼꼼하게 외우는 것도 좋습니다. 이런 방식으로 책을 읽다보면, 많은 단어를 빠르고 부담 없이 익히게 됩니다.

- **리딩할 때는 리딩에만 집중하자!** 원서를 읽는 중간 중간 모르는 단어가 나온다고 워크북을 들춰보거나, 곧바로 번역을 찾아보는 것은 매우 좋지 않은 습관입니다. 모르는 단어나 이해가 가지 않는 문장이 나온다고 해도 펜으로 가볍게 표시만 해두고, 전체적인 맥락을 잡아가며 빠르게 읽어나가세요. 리딩을 할 때는 속도에 대한 긴장감을 잃지 않으면서 리딩에만 집중하는 것이 좋습니다. 모르는 단어와 문장은, 리딩이 끝난 후에 한꺼번에 정리해보는 '리뷰' 시간을 갖습니다. 리뷰를 할 때는 번역은 물론 단어장과 사전도 꼼꼼하게 확인하면서 왜 이해가 되지 않았는지 확인해 봅니다.

- **번역 활용은 이렇게!** 이해가 가지 않는 문장은 번역을 통해서 그 의미를 파악할

수 있습니다. 하지만 한국어와 영어는 정확히 1:1 대응이 되지 않기 때문에 번역을 활용하는 데에도 지혜가 필요합니다. 의역이 된 부분까지 억지로 의미를 대응해서 암기하려고 하기보다, 어떻게 그런 의미가 만들어진 것인지 추측하면서 번역은 참고자료로 활용하는 것이 좋습니다.

- **듣기 훈련은 이렇게!** 리스닝 실력을 향상시키길 원한다면 오디오북을 적극적으로 활용하세요. 처음에는 오디오북을 틀어놓고 눈으로 해당 내용을 따라 읽으면서 훈련을 하고, 이것이 익숙해지면 오디오북만 틀어놓고 '귀를 통해' 책을 읽어보세요. 눈으로는 한 번도 읽지 않은 책을 귀를 통해 완벽하게 이해할 수 있다면 이후에는 영어 듣기로 고생하는 일은 거의 없을 것입니다.

- **소리 내어 읽고 녹음하자!** 이 책은 특히 소리 내어 읽기(Voice Reading)에 최적화된 문장 길이와 구조를 가지고 있습니다. 또한 오디오북 CD에 포함된 '따라 읽기용' 오디오북으로 소리 내어 읽기 훈련을 함께할 수 있습니다. 소리 내어 읽기를 하면서 내가 읽은 것을 녹음하고 들어보세요! 자신의 영어 발음을 들어보는 것은 몹시 민망한 일이지만, 그 과정을 통해서 의식적·무의식적으로 발음을 교정하게 됩니다. 이렇게 영어로 소리를 만들어 본 경험은 이후 탄탄한 스피킹 실력의 밑거름이 될 것입니다.

- **2~3번 반복해서 읽자!** 영어 초보자라면 2~3회 반복해서 읽을 것을 추천합니다. 초보자일수록 처음 읽을 때는 생소한 단어들과 스토리 때문에 내용 파악에 급급할 수밖에 없습니다. 하지만 일단 내용을 파악한 후에 다시 읽으면 어휘와 문장 구조 등 다른 부분까지 관찰하면서 조금 더 깊이 있게 읽을 수 있고, 그 과정에서 리딩 속도도 빨라지고 리딩 실력을 더 확고하게 다지게 됩니다.

- **'시리즈'로 꾸준히 읽자!** 한 작가의 책을 시리즈로 읽는 것 또한 영어 실력 향상에 큰 도움이 됩니다. 같은 등장인물이 다시 나오기 때문에 내용 파악이 더 수월할 뿐 아니라, 작가가 사용하는 어휘와 표현들도 자연스럽게 반복되기 때문에 탁월한 복습 효과까지 얻을 수 있습니다. 『아서 챕터북』 시리즈는 현재 10권, 총 50,000단어 분량이 출간되어 있습니다. 이 책들을 시리즈로 꾸준히 읽으면서 영어 실력을 쑥쑥 향상시켜 보세요!

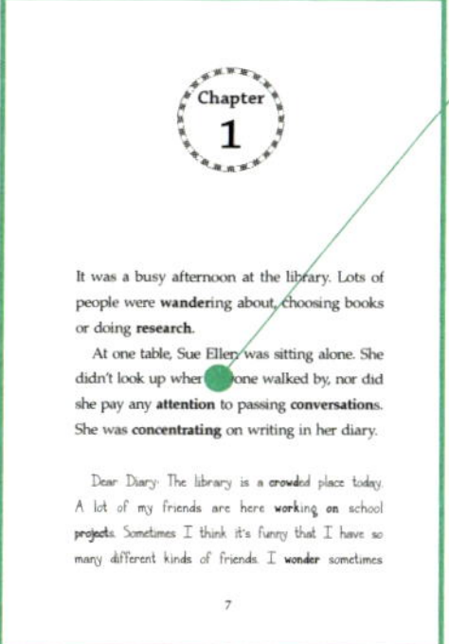

내용이 담긴 본문입니다.

원어민이 읽는 일반 원서와 같은 텍스트지만, 암기해
야 할 중요 어휘들은 볼드체로 표시되어 있습니다.
이 어휘들은 지금 들고 계신 워크북에 챕터별로 정리
되어 있습니다.

학습 심리학 연구 결과에 따르면, 한 단어씩 따로 외
우는 단어 암기는 거의 효과가 없다고 합니다. 대신
단어를 제대로 외우기 위해서는 문맥(Context) 속에
서 단어를 암기해야 하며, 한 단어 당 문맥 속에서 15
번 이상 마주칠 때 완벽하게 암기할 수 있다고 합니다.
이 책의 본문은 중요 어휘를 볼드로 강조하여, 문맥 속의 단어들을 더 확실히 인
지(Word Cognition in Context)하도록 돕고 있습니다. 또한 대부분의 중요한 단
어들은 다른 챕터에서도 반복해서 등장하기 때문에 이 책을 읽는 것만으로도 자
연스럽게 어휘력을 향상시킬 수 있습니다.

또한 본문에는 내용 이해를 돕기 위해 '각주'가 첨가
되어 있습니다. 각주는 굳이 암기할 필요는 없지만,
알아두면 내용을 더 깊이 있게 이해할 수 있어 원서
를 읽는 재미가 배가됩니다.

워크북(Workbook)의 구성

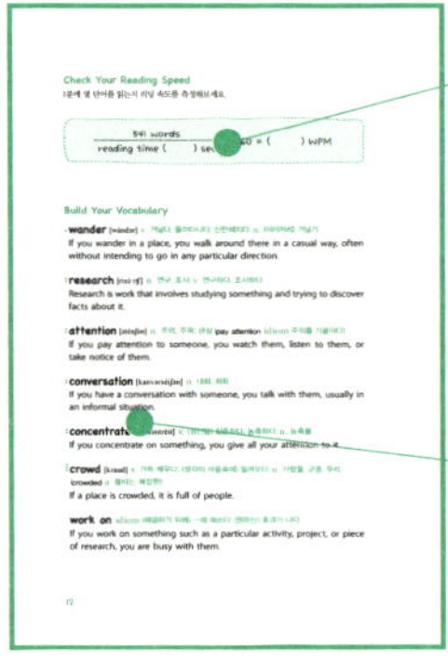

Check Your Reading Speed

해당 챕터의 단어 수가 기록되어 있어, 리딩 속도를 측정할 수 있습니다. 특히 리딩 속도를 중시하는 독자들이 유용하게 사용할 수 있습니다.

Build Your Vocabulary

본문에 볼드 표시되어 있는 단어들이 정리되어 있습니다. 리딩 전, 후에 반복해서 보면 원서를 더욱 쉽게 읽을 수 있고, 어휘력도 빠르게 향상됩니다.

단어는 〈빈도 – 스펠링 – 발음기호 – 품사 – 한글 뜻 – 영문 뜻〉 순서로 표기되어 있으며 빈도 표시(★)가 많을수록 필수 어휘입니다. 반복 등장하는 단어는 빈도 대신 '복습'으로 표기되어 있습니다. 품사는 아래와 같이 표기했습니다.

n. 명사 ｜ a. 형용사 ｜ ad. 부사 ｜ v. 동사

conj. 접속사 ｜ prep. 전치사 ｜ int. 감탄사 ｜ idiom 숙어 및 관용구

Comprehension Quiz

간단한 퀴즈를 통해 읽은 내용에 대한 이해력을 점검해 볼 수 있습니다.

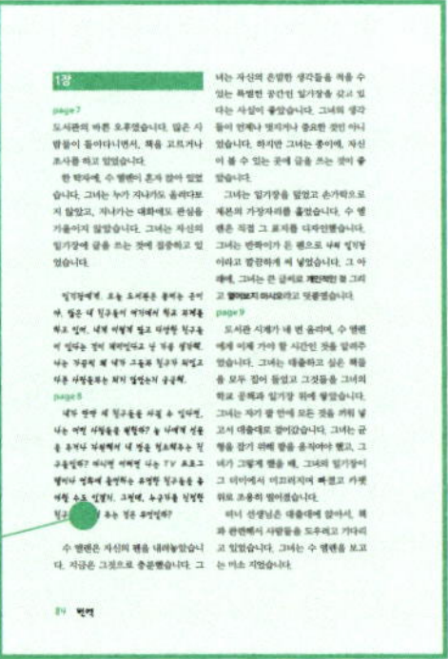

번역

영문과 비교할 수 있도록 최대한 직역에 가까운 번역을 담았습니다.

오디오북 CD 구성

이 책은 '듣기 훈련'과 '소리 내어 읽기 훈련'을
위한 2가지 종류의 오디오북이 포함되어 있습
니다.

- 듣기 훈련용 오디오북: 분당 145단어 속도
  (미국 현지 판매 중인 오디오북)
- 소리 내어 읽기 훈련용 오디오북: 분당 110
  단어 속도

오디오북은 MP3 파일로 제공되는 MP3 기기나
컴퓨터에 옮겨서 사용하셔야 합니다. 오디오북
에 이상이 있을 경우 helper@longtailbooks.co.kr로 메일을 주시면 자세한 안내를
받으실 수 있습니다.

EBS 동영상 강의 안내

EBS의 어학사이트(EBSlang.co.kr)에서 『아서 챕터북』 동영상 강의가 진행되고 있습니다.
영어 어순의 원리에 맞게 빠르고 정확하게 이해하는 법을 완벽하게 코치해주는 국내 유일의 강의!
저렴한 수강료에 완강 시 50% 환급까지!
지금 바로 열광적인 수강 평가와 샘플 강의를 확인하세요!

http://EBSreading.com

1. What was Sue Ellen doing at the library?

A. Using a computer to update her online diary

B. Looking for books for a school report

C. Studying together with her friends

D. Writing in her diary by herself

2. How did Sue Ellen feel about keeping a diary?

A. She thought it was hard work to write something every day.

B. She liked having a place to write down her private thoughts.

C. She thought that all of her ideas were great and important.

D. She thought writing a diary would make her popular at school.

3. **Which of the following was NOT true about Sue Ellen's diary?**

    A. Her mother had designed the cover.

    B. She had written PRIVATE in large letters.

    C. She had written My Diary neatly with a sparkle pen.

    D. She had written DO NOT OPEN in large letters.

4. **How did Sue Ellen lose her diary?**

    A. She accidentally put it on a shelf of books.

    B. She accidentally lost her diary in her backpack.

    C. She accidentally dropped her diary as she carried a pile of books.

    D. She accidentally left her diary on the table that she had been using.

5. **When did Sue Ellen notice that she had lost her diary?**

    A. She noticed it when she was checking out her books.

    B. She noticed it when a friend asked her about her diary.

    C. She noticed it when she was walking to the checkout counter.

    D. She noticed it when she wanted to write in it at home that evening.

Check Your Reading Speed

1분에 몇 단어를 읽는지 리딩 속도를 측정해보세요.

$$\frac{541 \text{ words}}{\text{reading time (} \quad \text{) sec}} \times 60 = (\quad) \text{ WPM}$$

Build Your Vocabulary

* **wander** [wándər] v. 거닐다, 돌아다니다; 산만해지다; n. (이리저리) 거닐기
If you wander in a place, you walk around there in a casual way, often without intending to go in any particular direction.

* **research** [risə́:rtʃ] n. 연구, 조사; v. 연구하다, 조사하다
Research is work that involves studying something and trying to discover facts about it.

* **attention** [əténʃən] n. 주의, 주목; 관심 (pay attention idiom 주의를 기울이다)
If you pay attention to someone, you watch them, listen to them, or take notice of them.

* **conversation** [kanvərséiʃən] n. 대화; 회화
If you have a conversation with someone, you talk with them, usually in an informal situation.

* **concentrate** [kánsəntrèit] v. (정신을) 집중하다; 농축하다; n. 농축물
If you concentrate on something, you give all your attention to it.

* **crowd** [kraud] v. 가득 메우다; (생각이 마음속에) 밀려오다; n. 사람들, 군중, 무리
(crowded a. 붐비는, 복잡한)
If a place is crowded, it is full of people.

work on idiom (해결하기 위해) ~에 애쓰다; (원하는) 효과가 나다
If you work on something such as a particular activity, project, or piece of research, you are busy with them.

project [prádʒekt] n. 과제; 계획, 기획; v. 계획하다; (빛·영상 등을) 비추다
A project is a detailed study of a subject by a pupil or student.

wonder [wʌ́ndər] v. 궁금해하다; (크게) 놀라다; n. 경탄, 경이
If you wonder about something, you think about it because it interests you and you want to know more about it.

volunteer [vàləntíər] v. 자원하다; n. 자원해서 하는 사람; 자원 봉사자
If you volunteer to do something, you offer to do it without being forced to do it.

star [sta:r] v. 주연을 맡다; 별표로 표시하다; n. 별; 스타; 주연
If an actor or actress stars in a play or film, he or she has one of the most important parts in it.

private [práivət] a. 은밀한; 사유의, 개인 소유의; 사적인; 혼자 있을 수 있는
Your private thoughts or feelings are ones that you do not talk about to other people.

trace [treis] v. (형체·윤곽을) 따라가다; 추적하다, 찾아내다; n. 자취, 흔적
If you trace something such as a pattern or a shape, for example with your finger or toe, you mark its outline on a surface.

edge [edʒ] n. 끝, 가장자리; 우위; v. 조금씩 움직이다
The edge of something is the place or line where it stops, or the part of it that is furthest from the middle.

binding [báindiŋ] n. (제본용) 표지; (천의) 가장자리 장식
The binding of a book is its cover.

design [dizáin] v. 도안하다; 설계하다; n. 디자인; 설계; 무늬
When someone designs a garment, building, machine, or other object, they plan it and make a detailed drawing of it from which it can be built or made.

cover [kʌ́vər] n. (책이나 잡지의) 표지; 덮개; v. 씌우다, 가리다; 덮다
The cover of a book or a magazine is the outside part of it.

print [print] v. (글자를) 인쇄체로 쓰다; 인쇄하다; (책·신문 등을) 찍다; n. (인쇄된) 활자

If you print words, you write in letters that are not joined together and that look like the letters in a book or newspaper.

neat [ni:t] a. 깔끔한; 정돈된, 단정한 (neatly ad. 깔끔하게; 솜씨 있게)

A neat object, part of the body, or shape is quite small and has a smooth outline.

sparkle [spa:rkl] n. 반짝거림, 광채; v. 반짝이다; 생기 넘치다

Sparkles are small points of light caused by light reflecting off a clear bright surface.

letter [létər] n. 글자, 문자; 편지; v. 글자가 들어 있다; 글자를 쓰다

Letters are written symbols which represent one of the sounds in a language.

strike [straik] v. (struck–stricken/struck) (시계가) 치다; 부딪치다; n. 파업; 공격

When a clock strikes, its bells make a sound to indicate what the time is.

remind [rimáind] v. 상기시키다, 다시 한 번 알려 주다

If someone reminds you of a fact or event that you already know about, they say something which makes you think about it.

check out idiom (도서관 등에서) 대출받다

If you check out, you borrow something such as a book or a video from a library.

pile [pail] v. 쌓다, 포개다; (많은 사람들이) 우르르 가다; n. 쌓아 놓은 것; 더미, 무더

If you pile things somewhere, you put them there so that they form a pile.

tuck [tʌk] v. 집어 넣다, 끼워 넣다; 밀어 넣다, 접다; n. 주름, 단

If you tuck something somewhere, you put it there so that it is safe, comfortable, or neat.

circulate [sə́:rkjulèit] v. (책이) 대출 가능하다; 순환하다 (circulation n. (도서의) 대출)

A circulation can refer to a book loan, as from a library lending department.

shift [ʃift] v. 이동하다, 옮기다; (견해·태도·방식을) 바꾸다; n. 변화
If you shift something or if it shifts, it moves slightly.

balance [bǽləns] v. 균형을 유지하다; 균형을 이루다; n. 균형, 평형
If you balance something somewhere, or if it balances there, it remains
steady and does not fall.

slip [slip] v. 빠져 나가다; 미끄러지다; 슬며시 가다; n. (작은) 실수; 미끄러짐
If something slips, it slides out of place or out of your hand.

counter [káuntər] n. (은행·상점 등의) 계산대, 판매대; v. 반박하다; a. 반대의
(checkout counter n. 계산대)
In a place such as a shop or café a counter is a long narrow table or flat
surface at which customers are served.

impress [imprés] v. 깊은 인상을 주다, 감명을 주다; 새기다 (impressive a. 인상적인)
Something that is impressive impresses you, for example because it is
great in size or degree, or is done with a great deal of skill.

make up one's mind idiom (마음을) 정하다, 결심하다
If you make up your mind or make your mind up, you decide which of
a number of possible things you will have or do.

admit [ædmít] v. 인정하다, 시인하다
If you admit that something bad, unpleasant, or embarrassing is true,
you agree, often unwillingly, that it is true.

spread [spred] v. (spread-spread) 펼치다; 펼쳐지다; 확산시키다; n. 확산, 전파; 길이
If you spread something somewhere, you open it out or arrange it over
a place or surface, so that all of it can be seen or used easily.

expect [ikspékt] v. 예상하다, 기대하다; 요구하다
If you expect something to happen, you believe that it will happen.

immediate [imí:diət] a. 즉각적인; 당면한 (immediately ad. 즉시, 즉각)
If something happens immediately, it happens without any delay.

search [səːrtʃ] v. 찾아보다, 뒤지다, 수색하다; n. 찾기, 수색
If you search for something or someone, you look carefully for them.

⋆ **clip** [klip] n. 핀, 클립; (짧게) 깎음; v. 클립으로 고정하다; 깎다 (paper clip n. 종이 집게)
A clip is a small device, usually made of metal or plastic, that is specially
shaped for holding things together.

⋆ **erase** [iréis] v. (지우개 등으로) 지우다; (완전히) 지우다 (eraser n. 고무 지우개)
An eraser is an object, usually a piece of rubber or plastic, which is used
for removing something that has been written using a pencil or a pen.

retrace [ri:tréis] v. (왔던 길을) 되짚어 가다; (사람의 행적을) 추적하다
If you retrace your steps or retrace your way, you return to the place you
started from by going back along the same route.

step [step] n. (발)걸음; 단계; 계단; v. (발걸음을 떼어놓아) 움직이다
If you take a step, you lift your foot and put it down in a different place,
for example when you are walking.

disappear [dìsəpíər] v. 사라지다, 보이지 않게 되다; 실종되다, 없어지다
If you say that someone or something disappears, you mean that you can
no longer see them, usually because you or they have changed position.

⋆ **kneel** [ni:l] v. (knelt–knelt) 무릎을 꿇다
When you kneel, you bend your legs so that your knees are touching
the ground.

⋆ **ouch** [autʃ] int. 아야 (하고 갑자기 아파서 내지르는 소리)
'Ouch!' is used in writing to represent the noise that people make when
they suddenly feel pain.

waste [weist] n. 쓰레기; 낭비; v. (돈·시간 등을) 낭비하다; 헛되이 쓰다
(wastebasket n. 휴지통)
A waste basket is a container for rubbish, especially paper, which is
usually placed on the floor in the corner of a room or next to a desk.

Chapter 2

1. **How did Ms. Turner know that Sue Ellen was upset?**

   A. She suddenly got very silent.

   B. She ran away from the checkout counter crying.

   C. Her face was red and her eyes were watery.

   D. She accidentally knocked over a pile of books.

2. **How did Ms. Turner tell Sue Ellen that she would help her?**

   A. She offered to make a poster to help her find her diary.

   B. She would tell everyone on the staff to be on the lookout.

   C. She would send an announcement out to the principal.

   D. She offered to buy her a new notebook to start a new diary.

3. **Why did Sue Ellen think Francine was laughing?**

    A. She thought she was reading a joke book.

    B. She thought she was reading her diary.

    C. She thought she had just heard a funny joke.

    D. She thought that she was trying to trick her.

4. **What was Francine reading?**

    A. A joke book

    B. Sue Ellen's diary

    C. The daily news

    D. Her homework assignment

5. **Why was Francine interested in Sue Ellen's diary?**

    A. Francine wanted to share Sue Ellen's secrets with her class.

    B. Sue Ellen said she had written mean things about Francine.

    C. Sue Ellen was Francine's best friend and she wanted to help her.

    D. Sue Ellen said she had written stuff about everyone.

1분에 몇 단어를 읽는지 리딩 속도를 측정해보세요.

$$\frac{474 \text{ words}}{\text{reading time (} \qquad \text{) sec}} \times 60 = (\qquad) \text{ WPM}$$

Build Your Vocabulary

★**drag** [dræg] v. 힘들게 움직이다; 끌다; (원치 않는 곳에) 가게 하다; n. 끌기; 장애물

If you say that you drag yourself somewhere, you are emphasizing that you have to make a very great effort to go there.

복습**check out** idiom (도서관 등에서) 대출받다

If you check out, you borrow something such as a book or a video from a library.

복습**counter** [káuntər] n. (은행·상점 등의) 계산대, 판매대; v. 반박하다; a. 반대의

(checkout counter n. 계산대)

In a place such as a shop or café a counter is a long narrow table or flat surface at which customers are served.

watery [wɔ́:təri] a. 물기가 많은, 물 같은; 희미한; 묽은

Something that is watery contains, resembles, or consists of water.

★**scan** [skæn] v. (유심히) 살피다; 훑어보다; n. 정밀 검사; 훑어보기

When you scan a place or group of people, you look at it carefully, usually because you are looking for something or someone.

★**assure** [əʃúər] v. 장담하다, 확언하다; 확인하다

If you assure someone that something is true or will happen, you tell them that it is definitely true or will definitely happen.

✲**describe** [diskráib] v. 묘사하다, 말하다, 서술하다; 형성하다

If you describe a person, object, event, or situation, you say what they are like or what happened.

⁑ **breath** [breθ] n. 숨, 입김 (take a deep breath idiom 심호흡하다)
When you take a deep breath, you breathe in a lot of air at one time.

⁎ **shiny** [ʃáini] a. 빛나는, 반짝거리는
Shiny things are bright and reflect light.

⁑ **leather** [léðər] n. 가죽
Leather is treated animal skin which is used for making shoes, clothes,
bags, and furniture.

복습 **cover** [kʌ́vər] n. (책이나 잡지의) 표지; 덮개; v. 씌우다, 가리다; 덮다
The cover of a book or a magazine is the outside part of it.

복습 **sparkle** [spa:rkl] n. 반짝거림, 광채; v. 반짝이다; 생기 넘치다
Sparkles are small points of light caused by light reflecting off a clear
bright surface.

복습 **letter** [létər] n. 글자, 문자; 편지; v. 글자가 들어 있다; 글자를 쓰다
Letters are written symbols which represent one of the sounds in a
language.

복습 **private** [práivət] a. 사유의, 개인 소유의; 사적인; 은밀한; 혼자 있을 수 있는
Your private things belong only to you, or may only be used by you.

⁎ **specific** [spisífik] a. 구체적인, 명확한, 분명한; 특정한
If someone is specific, they give a description that is precise and exact.
You can also use specific to describe their description.

복습 **search** [səːrʧ] n. 찾기, 수색; v. 찾아보다, 뒤지다, 수색하다
A search is an attempt to find something or someone by looking for
them carefully.

⁎ **staff** [stæf] n. 직원; v. 직원으로 일하다
The staff of an organization are the people who work for it.

be on the lookout idiom (~이 있는지) 세심히 살피다
If you are on the lookout for someone or something, you are searching
for them.

pause [pɔːz] v. (말·일을 하다가) 잠시 멈추다; 정지시키다; n. 멈춤
If you pause while you are doing something, you stop for a short period
and then continue.

exact [igzǽkt] a. 정확한, 정밀한; 엄격한 (exactly ad. 정확히, 틀림없이; 맞아)
You use exactly before an amount, number, or position to emphasize
that it is no more, no less, or no different from what you are stating.

trace [treis] v. 추적하다, 찾아내다; (형체·윤곽을) 따라가다; n. 자취, 흔적
If you trace someone or something, you find them after looking for them.

hunch [hʌnʧ] v. (등을) 구부리다; n. 예감
If you hunch forward, you raise your shoulders, put your head down, and
lean forward, often because you are cold, ill, or unhappy.

march [maːrʧ] v. (단호한 태도로 급히) 걸어가다; 행진하다; n. 행군, 행진; 3월
If you say that someone marches somewhere, you mean that they walk
there quickly and in a determined, confident, or angry way.

nod [nad] v. (고개를) 끄덕이다, 끄덕여 나타내다; n. (고개를) 끄덕임
If you nod, you move your head downward and upward to show
agreement, understanding, or approval.

snatch [snæʧ] v. 와락 붙잡다, 잡아채다; 간신히 얻다; n. 잡아 뺏음, 강탈
If you snatch something or snatch at something, you take it or pull it
away quickly.

steal [stiːl] v. 훔치다, 도둑질하다
If you steal something from someone, you take it away from them
without their permission and without intending to return it.

joke [dʒouk] n. 우스개, 농담; v. 농담하다, 재미있는 이야기를 하다
A joke is something that is said or done to make you laugh, for example
a funny story.

mystery [místəri] n. 수수께끼, 미스터리; 신비, 불가사의
(mysterious a. 이해하기 힘든, 기이한)
Someone or something that is mysterious is strange and is not known
about or understood.

‡ **valuable** [vǽljuəbl] a. 소중한, 귀중한; 가치가 큰, 값비싼
If you describe something or someone as valuable, you mean that they
are very useful and helpful.

⁎ **stuff** [stʌf] n. 것(들), 물건; v. 채워 넣다; 쑤셔 넣다
You can use stuff to refer to things such as a substance, a collection of
things, events, or ideas, or the contents of something in a general way
without mentioning the thing itself by name.

‡ **matter** [mǽtər] v. 중요하다; 문제되다; n. 문제, 일; 물질; 상황
If you say that something does matter, you mean that it is important to
you because it does have an effect on you or on a particular situation.

⁎ **rush** [rʌʃ] v. 급히 움직이다, 서두르다; 재촉하다; n. 혼잡, 분주함; (감정이) 치밀어 오름
If you rush somewhere, you go there quickly.

Chapter 3

1. **What did Muffy tell Francine might be a reason for why Sue Ellen was upset about losing her diary?**
   A. Muffy told Francine that Sue Ellen might have written about her.
   B. Muffy told Francine that Sue Ellen might have been writing a story.
   C. Muffy told Francine that Sue Ellen wrote down her ideas for school reports.
   D. Muffy told Francine that Sue Ellen wrote down her own embarrassing secrets.

2. **What was the mean thing that Muffy said Sue Ellen might have thought Francine did?**
   A. Francine pushed Sue Ellen off of her bike.
   B. Francine stole and ate Sue Ellen's lunch.

C. Francine pushed Sue Ellen in the mud.

D. Francine broke Sue Ellen's bike.

3. **Why had Francine laughed at Sue Ellen?**

   A. She thought it was funny that Sue Ellen was so upset.

   B. She thought it was funny that Sue Ellen lost her diary.

   C. She thought it was funny that Sue Ellen and Muffy were
      friends.

   D. She thought it was funny that Sue Ellen was covered in mud.

4. **What did Francine imagine Sue Ellen doing?**

   A. She imagined Sue Ellen going to the police about Francine.

   B. She imagined Sue Ellen going to her parents about Francine.

   C. She imagined Sue Ellen going to the doctor about Francine.

   D. She imagined Sue Ellen going to the principal about Francine.

5. **What disease was Francine diagnosed as having?**

   A. Ogre-ism

   B. Mean-ism

   C. Bully-itis

   D. Anger-ism

Check Your Reading Speed

1분에 몇 단어를 읽는지 리딩 속도를 측정해보세요.

$$\frac{555 \text{ words}}{\text{reading time (} \quad \text{) sec}} \times 60 = (\quad) \text{ WPM}$$

Build Your Vocabulary

* **hip** [hip] n. 허리; 둔부, 엉덩이
Your hips are the two areas at the sides of your body between the tops of your legs and your waist.

* **mean** [miːn] a. 못된, 심술궂은; 사나운; v. 의미하다; 의도하다
If someone is being mean, they are being unkind to another person, for example by not allowing them to do something.

* **fold** [fould] v. (두 손·팔 등을) 끼다; 접다; 감싸다; n. 주름; 접는 부분
If you fold your arms or hands, you bring them together and cross or link them, for example over your chest.

* **mud** [mʌd] n. 진흙, 진창
Mud is a sticky mixture of earth and water.

* **insist** [insíst] v. 고집하다, 주장하다, 우기다
If you insist that something is the case, you say so very firmly and refuse to say otherwise, even though other people do not believe you.

* **trip** [trip] v. 발을 헛디디다; ~를 넘어뜨리다; n. 여행; 발을 헛디딤
If you trip when you are walking, you knock your foot against something and fall or nearly fall.

* **cross** [krɔːs] v. 서로 겹치게 놓다; 가로지르다; 거스르다; n. 십자 기호, 십자가
If you cross your arms, legs, or fingers, you put one of them on top of the other.

28

* **afterward** [ǽftərwərd] ad. 나중에, 그 뒤에
If you do something or if something happens afterward, you do it or it happens after a particular event or time that has already been mentioned.

‡ **bite** [bait] v. (bit-bitten) (이빨로) 물다; n. 물기; 한 입
If you bite something, you use your teeth to cut into it, for example in order to eat it or break it.

* **beard** [biərd] n. (턱)수염 (bearded a. 수염이 있는)
A man's beard is the hair that grows on his chin and cheeks.

‡ **knock** [nak] n. 문 두드리는 소리; 부딪침; v. 치다; 부딪치다; (문을) 두드리다
A knock is a sudden short noise, which is made when someone or something hits a surface.

spatter [spǽtər] v. (액체 방울 등을) 튀기다; 후두두 떨어지다; n. (액체 등이) 튀는 것
If a liquid spatters a surface or you spatter a liquid over a surface, drops of the liquid fall on an area of the surface.

‡ **appointment** [əpɔ́intmənt] n. 약속; 임명, 지명
If you have an appointment with someone, you have arranged to see them at a particular time.

복습 **admit** [ædmít] v. 인정하다, 시인하다
If you admit that something bad, unpleasant, or embarrassing is true, you agree, often unwillingly, that it is true.

at once idiom 즉시, 당장, 지체 없이; 동시에, 한꺼번에
If you do something at once, you do it immediately.

‡ **emergency** [imə́:rdʒənsi] n. 비상 (사태)
An emergency is an unexpected and difficult or dangerous situation, especially an accident, which happens suddenly and which requires quick action to deal with it.

‡ **nature** [néiʧər] n. 본질; 천성, 본성; 자연
The nature of something is its basic quality or character.

stroke [strouk] v. 쓰다듬다; 달래다; n. 쓰다듬기; 치기

If you stroke someone or something, you move your hand slowly and gently over them.

consult [kənsʌ́lt] v. 찾아보다, 참고하다; 상담하다

If you consult a book or a map, you look in it or look at it in order to find some information.

lead [li:d] ① v. 선두를 달리다; 지휘하다; 이끌다; n. 선두, 우세 (leading a. 가장 중요한) ② n. [광물] 납

The leading person or thing in a particular area is the one which is most important or successful.

specialist [spéʃəlist] n. 전문가, 전공자; 전문의

A specialist is a person who has a particular skill or knows a lot about a particular subject.

filling [fíliŋ] n. (파이 등 음식의) 소, 속; a. 포만감을 주는

The filling in something such as a cake, pie, or sandwich is a substance or mixture that is put inside it.

snack [snæk] n. 간단한 식사, 간식; v. 간식을 먹다

A snack is a simple meal that is quick to cook and to eat.

crust [krʌst] n. (파이의) 윗부분; (빵) 껍질; 딱딱한 층

A pie's crust is its cooked pastry.

sigh [sai] v. 한숨을 쉬다, 한숨짓다; n. 한숨; 탄식

When you sigh, you let out a deep breath, as a way of expressing feelings such as disappointment, tiredness, or pleasure.

afraid [əfréid] a. 걱정하는; 두려워하는, 겁내는

If you are afraid that something unpleasant will happen, you are worried that it may happen and you want to avoid it.

exhibit [igzíbit] v. (감정·특질 등을) 보이다; 전시하다; n. 전시품; 증거물

If someone or something shows a particular quality, feeling, or type of behavior, you can say that they exhibit it.

sign [sain] n. 징후, 흔적; 몸짓; v. 서명하다; 신호를 보내다
If there is a sign of something, there is something which shows that it exists or is happening.

acute [əkjúːt] a. 극심한; 급성의; (감각이) 예민한
You can use acute to indicate that an undesirable situation or feeling is very severe or intense.

exact [igzǽkt] a. 정확한, 정밀한; 엄격한 (exactly ad. 맞아; 정확히, 틀림없이)
If you say 'Exactly,' you are agreeing with someone or emphasizing the truth of what they say.

flicker [flíkər] v. (빛·불 등이) 깜박거리다; 실룩거리다; n. 깜박거림; 실룩거림
(flickering a. 깜박거리는)
If a light or flame flickers, it shines unsteadily.

appear [əpíər] v. 나타나다, 보이기 시작하다; ~인 것 같다
When someone or something appears, they move into a position where you can see them.

disease [dizíːz] n. 질병, 병, 질환
A disease is an illness which affects people, animals, or plants, for example one which is caused by bacteria or infection.

victim [víktim] n. 환자; 피해자, 희생자
A victim is someone who has suffered as a result of someone else's actions or beliefs, or as a result of unpleasant circumstances.

burst [bəːrst] v. (burst–burst) 불쑥 움직이다; 터지다, 파열하다;
n. (갑자기) 한바탕 ~을 함
To burst into or out of a place means to enter or leave it suddenly with a lot of energy or force.

point [pɔint] v. (손가락 등으로) 가리키다; (길을) 알려 주다; n. 의미; 요점
If you point at a person or thing, you hold out your finger toward them in order to make someone notice them.

✲ **further** [fɔ́:rðər] a. 더 이상의, 추가의; ad. 더; 더 멀리에; v. 발전시키다
A further thing, number of things, or amount of something is an additional thing, number of things, or amount.

✲ **uniform** [jú:nəfɔ̀:rm] n. 제복, 유니폼; a. 획일적인, 균일한 (uniformed a. 제복을 입은)
If you use uniformed to describe someone who does a particular job, you mean that they are wearing a uniform.

✲ **guard** [ga:rd] n. 경비 요원, 보초; v. 지키다, 보호하다, 경비를 보다
A guard is a specially organized group of people, such as soldiers or policemen, who protect or watch someone or something.

✲ **restrain** [ristréin] v. 저지하다, 제지하다; (감정 등을) 억누르다
If you restrain someone, you stop them from doing what they intended or wanted to do, usually by using your physical strength.

contagious [kəntéidʒəs] a. 전염되는, 전염성의; 전염병에 걸린
A disease that is contagious can be caught by touching people or things that are infected with it.

✲ **remove** [rimú:v] v. 치우다, 내보내다; 없애다, 제거하다
If you remove something from a place, you take it away.

✲ **besides** [bisáidz] ad. 게다가, 뿐만 아니라; prep. ~외에
Besides is used to emphasize an additional point that you are making, especially one that you consider to be important.

Chapter 4

1. **Why did Muffy think that Sue Ellen made up stories for her diary?**

    A. She thought that everyday events were boring.

    B. She thought that Sue Ellen wanted to be a famous author.

    C. She thought that Sue Ellen had a talent for writing stories.

    D. She thought that Sue Ellen wanted to live in a fantasy world.

2. **How did Muffy imagine herself in Sue Ellen's diary?**

    A. She imagined herself as a fire-breathing dragon.

    B. She imagined herself as a knight in a suit of armor.

    C. She imagined herself as a princess with a jeweled crown.

    D. She imagined herself as a girl in a plain dress with no jewelry.

3. **Why were the villagers coming toward Muffy and Sue Ellen?**

A. They were bringing them gifts.

B. They were running toward them for help.

C. They were angry with Muffy's way of ruling.

D. They were trying to protect the princess from the dragon.

4. **What happened to Sue Ellen when she tried to fight the dragon?**

A. She got burned by the dragon's fire.

B. She got stuck in the doorway.

C. She got kicked by the dragon.

D. She had trouble putting on her armor.

5. **How did Muffy stop the dragon?**

A. She gave the dragon her treasures.

B. She trapped it inside of the castle.

C. She spritzed the dragon with perfume.

D. She dumped a bucket of water on the dragon.

1분에 몇 단어를 읽는지 리딩 속도를 측정해보세요.

$$\frac{473 \text{ words}}{\text{reading time (} \quad \text{) sec}} \times 60 = (\quad) \text{ WPM}$$

Build Your Vocabulary

★ **blink** [bliŋk] v. 눈을 깜박이다; (불빛이) 깜박거리다; n. 눈을 깜박거림
When you blink or when you blink your eyes, you shut your eyes and very quickly open them again.

복습 **disease** [dizí:z] n. 질병, 병, 질환
A disease is an illness which affects people, animals, or plants, for example one which is caused by bacteria or infection.

★ **wipe** [waip] v. 닦다; 지우다; n. 닦기, 훔치기
If you wipe something, you rub its surface to remove dirt or liquid from it.

★ **forehead** [fɔ́:rhèd] n. 이마
Your forehead is the area at the front of your head between your eyebrows and your hair.

★★ **head** [hed] v. (특정 방향으로) 향하다; ~을 이끌다; n. 머리, 고개; 책임자
If you are heading for a particular place, you are going toward that place.

★ **fountain** [fáuntən] n. 분수; 원천 (water fountain n. 식수대)
A water fountain is a device which supplies water for people to drink in places such as streets, parks, or schools.

excitable [iksáitəbl] a. 흥분을 잘 하는
If you describe someone as excitable, you mean that they behave in a rather nervous way and become excited very easily.

pause [pɔːz] v. (말·일을 하다가) 잠시 멈추다; 정지시키다; n. 멈춤

If you pause while you are doing something, you stop for a short period and then continue.

lean [liːn] v. ~에 기대다; (몸을) 숙이다; 기울다; a. 호리호리한

If you lean on or against someone or something, you rest against them so that they partly support your weight.

shelf [ʃelf] n. 책꽂이, (책장의) 칸; 선반

A shelf is a flat piece which is attached to a wall or to the sides of a cupboard for keeping things on.

boring [bɔ́ːriŋ] a. 재미없는, 지루한

Someone or something boring is so dull and uninteresting that they make people tired and impatient.

make up idiom (이야기 등을) 만들어 내다; ~을 이루다, 형성하다

If you make up something, you invent something artificial or untrue, often in order to trick someone.

flow [flou] v. (흐르듯) 드리워지다; 흐르다; 계속 이동하다; n. 흐름; 이동
(flowing a. (의복·머리 등이) 풍성하게 늘어진)

If hair or clothing flows, it falls or moves in a smooth graceful way around someone's body.

jewel [dʒúːəl] n. 보석; 장신구 (jeweled a. 보석으로 장식한)

A jewel is a precious stone used to decorate valuable things that you wear, such as rings or necklaces.

crown [kraun] n. 왕관; 왕위, 왕권; v. 왕관을 씌우다, 왕위에 앉히다

A crown is a circular ornament, usually made of gold and jewels, which a king or queen wears on their head at official ceremonies.

plain [plein] a. 소박한, 꾸미지 않은; 분명한; n. 평원, 평지

Something that is plain is very simple in style.

jewelry [dʒúːəlri] n. 장신구, 보석 장식; 보석류

Jewelry is ornaments which people wear, and which is often made of a valuable metal and decorated with precious stones.

* **compare** [kəmpέər] v. 필적하다, 비교가 되다; 비교하다; 비유하다
If you say that something does not compare with something else, you mean that it is much worse.

go on idiom 말을 계속하다; (어떤 상황이) 계속되다; 시작하다
When you go on, you continue speaking after a short pause.

* **fair** [fɛər] a. 아름다운; 공정한; 타당한; n. 박람회
If someone, especially a woman is fair, she is beautiful.

* **hide** [haid] v. (hid-hidden) (보이지 않도록) 가리다; 감추다, 숨기다; 숨다
If something hides an object, it covers it and prevents it from being seen.

* **dare** [dɛər] v. 감히 ～하다, ～할 엄두를 내다; 해 보라고 부추기다; n. 모험, 도전
If you dare to do something, you do something which requires a lot of courage.

* **interrupt** [ìntərʌ́pt] v. 차단하다; (말·행동을) 가로막다, 방해하다; 중단시키다
If something interrupts a line, surface, or view, it stops it from being continuous or makes it look irregular.

* **gasp** [gæsp] v. 숨이 턱 막히다, 헉 하고 숨을 쉬다; n. 헉 하는 소리를 냄
When you gasp, you take a short quick breath through your mouth, especially when you are surprised, shocked, or in pain.

* **breathe** [bri:ð] v. 호흡하다, 숨을 쉬다 (fire-breathing a. 불을 뿜는)
When they breathe smoke or a particular kind of air, they take it into their lungs and let it out again as they breathe.

* **village** [vílidʒ] n. 마을, 부락, 촌락 (villager n. 마을 사람)
A village consists of a group of houses, together with other buildings such as a church and a school, in a country area.

* **comb** [koum] v. 빗다, 빗질하다; 샅샅이 찾다; n. 빗
When you comb your hair, you tidy it using a comb.

alarm [əláːrm] v. 불안하게 하다; 경보장치를 달다; n. 불안, 공포; 경보 장치
(alarmed a. 불안해하는, 두려워하는)
If someone is alarmed, they feel afraid or anxious that something unpleasant or dangerous might happen.

sigh [sai] v. 한숨을 쉬다, 한숨짓다; n. 한숨; 탄식
When you sigh, you let out a deep breath, as a way of expressing feelings such as disappointment, tiredness, or pleasure.

suit [suːt] n. (특정한 활동 때 입는) 옷, 복; 정장; v. 어울리다; 편리하다
A particular type of suit is a piece of clothing that you wear for a particular activity.

armor [áːrmər] n. 갑옷, 철갑; 무기; v. ~에게 갑옷을 입히다
Armor is a defensive covering, as of metal, wood, or leather, worn to protect the body against weapons.

handle [hændl] v. 다루다, 처리하다; (차량 등이) 말을 잘 듣다; n. 손잡이
If you say that someone can handle a problem or situation, you mean that they have the ability to deal with it successfully.

clank [klæŋk] v. 철커덕 하는 소리가 나다
When large metal objects clank, they make a noise because they are hitting together or hitting against something hard.

matter [mætər] n. 문제, 일; 물질; 상황; v. 중요하다; 문제되다
You use matter in expressions such as 'What's the matter?' or 'Is anything the matter?' when you think that someone has a problem and you want to know what it is.

stick [stik] v. 꼼짝하지 않다; 찔러 넣다; 고수하다; n. 막대 (stuck a. 꼼짝 못하는)
If something is stuck in a particular position, it is fixed tightly in this position and is unable to move.

doorway [dɔ́ːrwèi] n. 출입구, 현관
A doorway is a space in a wall where a door opens and closes.

★ **braid** [breid] v. (머리·밧줄 등을) 땋다, 꼬다; n. (머리 등을) 땋은 것
(braided a. (머리를) 땋은)
If you braid hair or a group of threads, you twist three or more lengths of
the hair or threads over and under each other to make one thick length.

‡ **thread** [θred] v. (실 등을) 꿰다; 요리조리 빠져나가다; n. 실; (이야기 등의) 맥락
If you thread a long thin object through something, you pass it through
one or more holes or narrow spaces.

★ **handy** [hǽndi] a. 가까운 곳에 있는; 유용한, 편리한
A thing or place that is handy is nearby and therefore easy to get or
reach.

pulley [púli] n. 도르래
A pulley is a device consisting of a wheel over which a rope or chain is
pulled in order to lift heavy objects.

‡ **prepare** [pripέər] v. 준비하다; 대비하다, 각오하다
If you prepare something, you make it ready for something that is going
to happen.

★ **toast** [toust] v. (구워서) 노릇노릇하게 하다; 건배하다; n. 토스트; 건배
When you toast something such as bread, you cook it at a high
temperature so that it becomes brown and crisp.

★ **crisp** [krisp] n. 바삭바삭한 것; 감자 칩; a. 바삭바삭한; 빳빳한; v. 바삭바삭하게 만들다
(burn to a crisp idiom 바싹 태우다)
If you burn someone or something to a crisp, you burn something
completely, leaving only a charred remnant.

spritz [spritz] v. (아주 작은 물방울 등을) 뿌리다
If you spritz a liquid, you squirt or spray a liquid at or on to something
in quick, short bursts.

★ **perfume** [pə́:rfju:m] n. 향수; 향기, 향내
Perfume is a pleasant-smelling liquid which women put on their skin to
make themselves smell nice.

snuff [snʌf] v. (촛불을) 끄다; 냄새를 맡다; n. 코로 들이쉬기; 냄새
If you snuff out something like a candle or flame, you extinguish it.

gush [gʌʃ] v. (칭찬·감정을) 마구 표현하다; (액체가) 솟구치다; n. (액체의) 분출
If someone gushes, they express their admiration or pleasure in an exaggerated way.

repay [ripéi] v. (은혜 등을) 갚다, 보답하다; (빌린 돈을) 갚다
If you repay a favor that someone did for you, you do something for them in return.

practical [prǽktikəl] a. 현실적인, 실리적인; 현실성 있는, 실현 가능한; 실용적인
You describe people as practical when they make sensible decisions and deal effectively with problems.

suppose [səpóuz] v. (~이라고) 생각하다, 추측하다; 가정하다
If you suppose that something is true, you believe that it is probably true, because of other things that you know.

Chapter 5

1. Why did Binky want Muffy's attention?

A. He wanted to stop her from knocking over a bookshelf.

B. He wanted to tell her that she was blocking a bookshelf.

C. He wanted to tell her that he had found Sue Ellen's diary.

D. He wanted to ask her to help search for Sue Ellen's diary.

2. What did Binky do with Sue Ellen's diary?

A. He brought it back to Sue Ellen.

B. He tore out a page about him.

C. He put it in his backpack.

D. He put it on a cart.

3. What did Binky think about writing a diary?

    A. He thought that it was something that he wanted to try.

    B. He thought that it was dangerous if someone lost their diary.

    C. He thought that it was a lot of work and didn't appeal to him.

    D. He thought that it was something that girls did more than boys.

4. How did Binky imagine Sue Ellen thinking of him?

    A. He imagined that she was afraid of him.

    B. He imagined that she thought that he was a bully.

    C. He imagined that she thought he was the man of her dreams.

    D. He imagined that she thought the other boys were afraid of him.

5. Which of the following was NOT a way that Binky imagined Sue Ellen trying to get his attention?

    A. Singing a special song for him in class

    B. Following him around the playground

    C. Bringing him extra desserts for lunch

    D. Smiling at him a lot

Check Your Reading Speed

1분에 몇 단어를 읽는지 리딩 속도를 측정해보세요.

$$\frac{504 \text{ words}}{\text{reading time ( ) sec}} \times 60 = (\quad) \text{ WPM}$$

Build Your Vocabulary

* **tap** [tæp] v. (가볍게) 톡톡 두드리다; n. (가볍게) 두드리기; 수도꼭지

If you tap something, you hit it with a quick light blow or a series of quick light blows.

복습 **blink** [bliŋk] v. 눈을 깜박이다; (불빛이) 깜박거리다; n. 눈을 깜박거림

When you blink or when you blink your eyes, you shut your eyes and very quickly open them again.

* **shrug** [ʃrʌg] v. (어깨를) 으쓱하다; n. (어깨를) 으쓱하기

If you shrug, you raise your shoulders to show that you are not interested in something or that you do not know or care about something.

** **block** [blak] v. 막다, 차단하다; 방해하다; n. 사각형 덩어리; 구역, 블록

If you block someone's way, you prevent them from going somewhere or entering a place by standing in front of them.

복습 **shelf** [ʃelf] n. 책꽂이, (책장의) 칸; 선반

A shelf is a flat piece which is attached to a wall or to the sides of a cupboard for keeping things on.

복습 **step** [step] v. (발걸음을 떼어놓아) 움직이다; n. (발)걸음; 단계; 계단

If you step on something or step in a particular direction, you put your foot on the thing or move your foot in that direction.

* **aside** [əsáid] ad. 한쪽으로; (길을) 비켜; (나중에 쓰려고) 따로

If you move aside, you get out of someone's way.

44

☆ **tough** [tʌf] a. 힘든, 어려운; 억센, 거친; 엄한 (tough luck idiom 거 참 운도 없군)
You say 'tough luck' to someone to show sympathy for something unfortunate that has happened to them.

☆ **confuse** [kənfjúːz] v. (사람을) 혼란시키다; 혼동하다 (confused a. 혼란스러워 하는)
If you are confused, you do not know exactly what is happening or what to do.

복습 **private** [práivət] a. 사유의, 개인 소유의; 사적인; 은밀한; 혼자 있을 수 있는
Your private things belong only to you, or may only be used by you.

☆ **cart** [kaːrt] n. 손수레, 카트; v. (수레나 차량으로) 운반하다; 손으로 들어 나르다
A cart is a shallow open container on wheels that may be pulled or pushed by hand.

복습 **nod** [nad] v. (고개를) 끄덕이다, 끄덕여 나타내다; n. (고개를) 끄덕임
If you nod, you move your head downward and upward to show agreement, understanding, or approval.

복습 **point** [pɔint] n. 요점; 의미; v. (손가락 등으로) 가리키다; (길을) 알려 주다
The point of what you are saying or discussing is the most important part that provides a reason or explanation for the rest.

복습 **search** [səːrʧ] n. 찾기, 수색; v. 찾아보다, 뒤지다, 수색하다
A search is an attempt to find something or someone by looking for them carefully.

복습 **impress** [imprés] v. 깊은 인상을 주다, 감명을 주다; 새기다 (impressed a. 감명을 받은)
If something impresses you, you feel great admiration for it.

☆ **appeal** [əpíːl] v. 관심을 끌다, 매력적이다; 호소하다; n. 매력; 호소; 간청
If something appeals to you, you find it attractive or interesting.

☆ **reach** [riːʧ] v. (손·팔을) 뻗다, 내밀다; 이르다, 도달하다; n. 거리; 범위
If you reach somewhere, you move your arm and hand to take or touch something.

⁑**freeze** [friːz] v. (froze–frozen) (두려움 등으로 몸이) 얼어붙다; 얼(리)다; n. 동결; 한파
If someone who is moving freezes, they suddenly stop and become completely still and quiet.

midair [midέər] n. 공중, 상공
If something happens in midair, it happens in the air, rather than on the ground.

⁑**include** [inklúːd] v. 포함하다, 포함시키다
If one thing includes another thing, it has the other thing as one of its parts.

⁑**realize** [ríːəlàiz] v. 깨닫다, 알아차리다; 실현하다
If you realize that something is true, you become aware of that fact or understand it.

⁑**draw** [drɔː] v. (drew–drawn) 그리다; (사람의 마음을) 끌다; n. 추첨, 제비 뽑기
When you draw, or when you draw something, you use a pencil or pen to produce a picture, pattern, or diagram.

⁎**margin** [máːrdʒin] n. (책 페이지의) 여백; 차이; 여유
The margin of a written or printed page is the empty space at the side of the page.

복습**stick** [stik] v. 꼼짝하지 않다; 찔러 넣다; 고수하다; n. 막대 (stuck a. 꼼짝 못하는)
If something is stuck in a particular position, it is fixed tightly in this position and is unable to move.

복습**mud** [mʌd] n. 진흙, 진창
Mud is a sticky mixture of earth and water.

복습**volunteer** [vàləntíər] v. 자원하다; n. 자원해서 하는 사람; 자원 봉사자
If you volunteer to do something, you offer to do it without being forced to do it.

⁑**lift** [lift] v. 들어 올리다, 올리다; n. (들어)올리기; (차 등을) 태워 주기
If you lift something, you move it to another position, especially upward.

necessary [nésəsèri] a. 필요한; 필연적인, 불가피한
Something that is necessary is needed in order for something else to happen.

mind [maind] v. 상관하다, 신경 쓰다; n. 마음, 정신; 관심
If you do not mind something, you are not annoyed or bothered by it.

look up to idiom ~를 우러러보다, ~을 존경하다
If you look up to someone, you admire or respect them.

blame [bleim] v. ~을 탓하다, ~의 책임으로 보다; n. 책임; 탓
If you blame a person or thing for something bad, you believe or say that they are responsible for it or that they caused it.

notice [nóutis] v. ~을 의식하다; 주목하다; n. 주목; 안내문
If you notice something or someone, you become aware of them.

playground [pléigraund] n. (학교의) 운동장, (공원의) 놀이터
A playground is a piece of land, at school or in a public area, where children can play.

dessert [dizə́:rt] n. 디저트, 후식
Dessert is something sweet, such as fruit or a pudding, that you eat at the end of a meal.

attention [əténʃən] n. 관심; 주의, 주목
If someone or something is getting attention, they are being dealt with or cared for.

burp [bə:rp] v. 트림하다
When someone burps, they make a noise because air from their stomach has been forced up through their throat.

afterward [aéftərwərd] ad. 나중에, 그 뒤에
If you do something or if something happens afterward, you do it or it happens after a particular event or time that has already been mentioned.

^{복습}**go on** idiom (어떤 상황이) 계속되다; 말을 계속하다; 시작하다

If you say that you cannot go on like this, it means things cannot continue
to happen or exist without changing.

serenade [sèrənéid] v. 세레나데를 부르다; n. 세레나데

If one person serenades another, they sing or play a piece of music for
them.

Chapter 6

1. **Why did Arthur say that Binky looked like the Statue of Liberty?**

    A. He was wearing a robe.

    B. He was wearing green.

    C. He was holding a torch.

    D. He had his arm raised.

2. **Why had Binky not given Sue Ellen her diary back?**

    A. He had wanted to read it first.

    B. He hadn't known it was her diary.

    C. He had wanted to keep it hidden.

    D. He had wanted to show Arthur first.

3. **How did Arthur imagine Sue Ellen feeling about his reading habits?**

    A. He imagined her thinking that he didn't read enough books.

    B. He imagined her thinking that he used the library too much.

    C. He imagined her thinking that he shouldn't read in the dark.

    D. He imagined her thinking that he read things that gave him nightmares.

4. **What did Arthur imagine Sue Ellen keeping track of in her diary?**

    A. The days that were left in the school year

    B. Her friend's personal problems

    C. Arthur's flaws

    D. Binky's smiles

5. **What was Number 78 on Sue Ellen's list?**

    A. Doesn't take criticism well

    B. Doesn't know how to keep organized

    C. Doesn't listen to friends

    D. Doesn't sit still

1분에 몇 단어를 읽는지 리딩 속도를 측정해보세요.

$$\frac{523 \text{ words}}{\text{reading time (} \qquad \text{) sec}} \times 60 = (\qquad) \text{ WPM}$$

Build Your Vocabulary

^{복습} **matter** [mǽtər] n. 문제, 일; 물질; 상황; v. 중요하다; 문제되다

You use matter in expressions such as 'What's the matter?' or 'Is anything the matter?' when you think that someone has a problem and you want to know what it is.

drop [drap] v. 떨어뜨리다; 약해지다, 낮추다; n. 방울; 하락, 감소

If a person drops a part of their body to a lower position, they move to that position, often in a tired and lifeless way.

load [loud] v. 가득 안겨 주다; (짐·사람 등을) 싣다; n. 짐, 화물
(load down idiom (무거운 것을) 잔뜩 들게 하다)

If you load someone or something down with things, you give them too many things to carry.

stack [stæk] n. 무더기, 더미; (pl.) (도서관의) 서가; v. 쌓다, 포개다; 채우다

A stack of things is a pile of them.

strange [streindʒ] a. 이상한; 낯선

Something that is strange is unusual or unexpected, and makes you feel slightly nervous or afraid.

^{복습} **lift** [lift] v. 들어 올리다, 올리다; n. (들어)올리기; (차 등을) 태워 주기

If you lift something, you move it to another position, especially upward.

never mind idiom (중요하지 않으니까) 신경 쓰지 마, 괜찮아

You use 'never mind' to tell someone not to do something or worry about something, because it is not important.

subject [sʌ́bdʒikt] n. 주제, 화제; 과목; a. ~에 달려 있는; v. 지배하에 두다
The subject of something such as a conversation, letter, or book is the thing that is being discussed or written about.

cart [ka:rt] n. 손수레, 카트; v. (수레나 차량으로) 운반하다; 손으로 들어 나르다
A cart is a shallow open container on wheels that may be pulled or pushed by hand.

frown [fraun] v. 얼굴을 찌푸리다; n. 찡그림, 찌푸림
When someone frowns, their eyebrows become drawn together, because they are annoyed or puzzled.

wonder [wʌ́ndər] v. 궁금해하다; (크게) 놀라다; n. 경탄, 경이
If you wonder about something, you think about it because it interests you and you want to know more about it.

shudder [ʃʌ́dər] v. (공포·추위 등으로) 몸을 떨다, 몸서리치다; n. 몸이 떨림, 전율
If you shudder, you shake with fear, horror, or disgust, or because you are cold.

expect [ikspékt] v. 예상하다, 기대하다; 요구하다
If you expect something to happen, you believe that it will happen.

odd [ad] a. 이상한, 특이한; 가끔의; 다양한
If you describe someone or something as odd, you think that they are strange or unusual.

cut off idiom ~을 차단하다; ~을 자르다
To cut off means to stop the supply of gas, water or electricity to someone's home.

supply [səplái] n. 공급, 제공; 비축(량); v. 공급하다, 제공하다
(blood supply n. 혈액 공급)
A supply of something is an amount of it which someone has or which is available for them to use.

public [pʌ́blik] n. 일반 사람들, 대중; a. 일반인의, 대중의; 대중을 위한, 공공의
If you say or do something in public, you say or do it when a group of people are present.

stuff [stʌf] n. 것(들), 물건; v. 채워 넣다; 쑤셔 넣다

You can use stuff to refer to things such as a substance, a collection of things, events, or ideas, or the contents of something in a general way without mentioning the thing itself by name.

hold back idiom (감정을) 누르다; ~을 비밀로 하다; 방해하다

If you hold back something, you stop yourself from expressing or showing how you feel.

mystery [místəri] n. 수수께끼, 미스터리; 신비, 불가사의

A mystery is something that is not understood or known about.

mummy [mʌ́mi] n. 미라

A mummy is a dead body which was preserved long ago by being rubbed with special oils and wrapped in cloth.

curse [kəːrs] n. 저주; 욕(설), 악담; v. 욕(설)을 하다; 저주를 내리다

If you say that there is a curse on someone, you mean that there seems to be a supernatural power causing unpleasant things to happen to them.

eerie [íəri] a. 괴상한, 으스스한

If you describe something as eerie, you mean that it seems strange and frightening, and makes you feel nervous.

canal [kənǽl] n. 운하, 수로

A canal is a long, narrow stretch of water that has been made for boats to travel along or to bring water to a particular area.

nightmare [náitmɛər] n. 악몽; 아주 끔찍한 일

A nightmare is a very frightening dream.

adventure [ædvénʧər] n. 모험; 모험심

If someone has an adventure, they become involved in an unusual, exciting, and rather dangerous journey or series of events.

fold [fould] v. (두 손·팔 등을) 끼다; 접다; 감싸다; n. 주름; 접는 부분

If you fold your arms or hands, you bring them together and cross or link them, for example over your chest.

in fact idiom 사실은, 실은; 실제로는
You use in fact to indicate that you are giving more detailed information about what you have just said.

improve [imprúːv] v. 개선되다, 나아지다; 향상시키다 (improvement n. 개선; 향상)
If there is an improvement in something, it becomes better.

keep track of idiom ~에 대해 계속 알고 있다, ~을 놓치지 않다
If you keep track of a situation or a person, you make sure that you have the newest and most accurate information about them all the time.

flaw [flɔː] n. 결점, 흠
A flaw in someone's character is an undesirable quality that they have.

organize [ɔ́ːrɡənàiz] v. 정리하다, 체계화하다; 준비하다, 조직하다
If you organize a set of things, you arrange them in an ordered way or give them a structure.

take action idiom ~에 대해 조치를 취하다, 행동에 옮기다
If you take action, you begin to do something to solve a particular problem.

shape up idiom 태도를 개선하다; (좋은 방향으로) 전개되다
If you shape up, you improve your behavior or your work.

scroll [skroul] n. 두루마리; v. 말다, 두루마리로 만들다
A scroll is a long roll of paper or a similar material with writing on it.

roll [roul] v. (둥글게) 말다; 구르다, 굴리다; n. 통, 두루마리; 구르기
(unroll v. (두루마리처럼 말린 것을) 펼치다)
If you unroll something such as a sheet of paper or cloth, it opens up and becomes flat when it was previously rolled in a cylindrical shape.

halfway [hǽfwei] ad. (거리·시간상으로) 중간에, 가운데쯤에
Halfway means in the middle of a place or between two points, at an equal distance from each of them.

복습**sigh** [sai] v. 한숨을 쉬다, 한숨짓다; n. 한숨; 탄식

When you sigh, you let out a deep breath, as a way of expressing feelings such as disappointment, tiredness, or pleasure.

skip [skip] v. 건너뛰다, 생략하다; 깡충깡충 뛰다; n. 깡충깡충 뛰기

If you skip or skip over a part of something you are reading or a story you are telling, you miss it out or pass over it quickly and move on to something else.

direct [dirékt] a. (중간에 제삼자나 매개물 없이) 직접적인; 직행의; v. ~로 향하다; 지휘하다, 총괄하다 (directly ad. 곧장, 똑바로)

Direct means moving towards a place or object, without changing direction and without stopping, for example in a journey.

복습**afraid** [əfréid] a. 두려워하는, 겁내는; 걱정하는

If you are afraid of someone or afraid to do something, you are frightened because you think that something very unpleasant is going to happen to you.

criticism [krítəsìzm] n. (좋지 못한 점을 지적하는) 비판, 비난; 비평, 평론

Criticism is the action of expressing disapproval of something or someone.

hunt [hʌnt] v. (찾기 힘든 것을) 찾다; 사냥하다; n. 수색, 추적; 사냥

If you hunt for something or someone, you try to find them by searching carefully or thoroughly.

slight [slait] a. 약간의, 조금의, 경미한 (slightly ad. 약간, 조금)

Slightly means to some degree but not to a very large degree.

dive [daiv] v. (dove/dived–dived) 휙 움직이다; (물 속으로) 뛰어들다; n. 다이빙, (물 속으로) 뛰어들기

If you dive in a particular direction or into a particular place, you jump or move there quickly.

복습**shelf** [ʃelf] n. (pl. shelves) 책꽂이, (책장의) 칸; 선반 (bookshelf n. (pl. bookshelves) 책꽂이)

A bookshelf is a shelf on which you keep books.

Chapter 7

1. **What did Arthur say he was trying to do when he crashed into the library assistant?**

   A. He said he was trying to escape.

   B. He said he was looking for a book.

   C. He said he was looking for a diary.

   D. He said he was hiding from someone.

2. **Which book in particular caught his attention in the books that he had knocked over?**

   A. One that looked like his diary

   B. One that said PRIVATE on the front

   C. One that said SUE ELLEN on the front

   D. One that said FRANCINE on the front

3. **What were Binky, Muffy, and Francine doing as a team?**

   A. They were trying to find Arthur.

   B. They were hiding from Sue Ellen.

   C. They were working on a school project.

   D. They were hunting for Sue Ellen's diary.

4. **How did Muffy react to Arthur asking about Sue Ellen?**

   A. She said she was busy.

   B. She told him to go away.

   C. She asked if he had found her diary.

   D. She told him to help her look for Sue Ellen's diary.

5. **Why did Arthur need to find Sue Ellen?**

   A. He needed her help.

   B. He had found her diary.

   C. He wanted to help her look for her diary.

   D. He needed her help with writing his own diary.

1분에 몇 단어를 읽는지 리딩 속도를 측정해보세요.

$$\frac{507 \text{ words}}{\text{reading time ( ) sec}} \times 60 = (\quad) \text{ WPM}$$

Build Your Vocabulary

watch out idiom 조심해라!
You say 'watch out,' when you warn someone about something dangerous.

assistant [əsístənt] n. 조수, 보조원; a. 보조의
Someone's assistant is a person who helps them in their work.

crash [kræʃ] v. 부딪치다; 충돌하다; 굉음을 내다; n. 요란한 소리; (자동차·항공기) 사고
If something crashes somewhere, it moves and hits something else violently, making a loud noise.

pick oneself up idiom (넘어졌다가) 일어서다
If you pick yourself up, you stand up again after a fall.

never mind idiom (중요하지 않으니까) 신경 쓰지 마, 괜찮아
You use 'never mind' to tell someone not to do something or worry about something, because it is not important.

mess [mes] n. (지저분하고) 엉망인 상태; 엉망인 상황; v. 엉망으로 만들다
If you say that something is a mess or in a mess, you think that it is in an untidy state.

tackle [tækl] v. 달려들다; (힘든 문제·상황과) 씨름하다; n. 태클; 연장; 도구
If you tackle someone, you attack them and fight them.

shrug [ʃrʌg] v. (어깨를) 으쓱하다; n. (어깨를) 으쓱하기
If you shrug, you raise your shoulders to show that you are not interested in something or that you do not know or care about something.

get one's eye on idiom ~을 눈여겨 보다; 경계하다
If you get your eye on someone or something, you watch them carefully.

gather [gǽðər] v. (여기저기 있는 것을) 모으다; (사람들이) 모이다
If you gather things, you collect them together so that you can use them.

subject [sʌ́bdʒikt] n. 주제, 화제; 과목; a. ~에 달려 있는; v. 지배하에 두다
The subject of something such as a conversation, letter, or book is the thing that is being discussed or written about.

particular [pərtíkjulər] a. 특별한; 특정한; n. 자세한 사실
You use in particular to indicate that what you are saying applies especially to one thing or person.

attention [əténʃən] n. 관심; 주의, 주목
(catch one's attention idiom ~의 관심을 사로잡다)
If someone or something catches your attention, you suddenly notice them.

hunt [hʌnt] v. (찾기 힘든 것을) 찾다; 사냥하다; n. 수색, 추적; 사냥
If you hunt for something or someone, you try to find them by searching carefully or thoroughly.

bookcase [búkkèis] n. 책장, 책꽂이, 서가
A bookcase is a piece of furniture with shelves that you keep books on.

on one's hands and knees idiom 넙죽 엎드려, 네 발로 기어서
If you are on your hands and knees, you are on the floor, with your hands and your lower legs on the ground.

give a look idiom ~를 보다, (어떤) 표정을 짓다
If you give someone a look, you look at them in a particular way.

insist [insíst] v. 고집하다, 주장하다, 우기다
If you insist that something is the case, you say so very firmly and refuse to say otherwise, even though other people do not believe you.

frown [fraun] v. 얼굴을 찌푸리다; n. 찡그림, 찌푸림
When someone frowns, their eyebrows become drawn together, because they are annoyed or puzzled.

unless [ənlés] prep. ~지 않는 한, ~이 아닌 한
You use unless to introduce the only circumstances in which an event you are mentioning will not take place or in which a statement you are making is not true.

gasp [gæsp] v. 숨이 턱 막히다, 헉 하고 숨을 쉬다; n. 헉 하는 소리를 냄
When you gasp, you take a short quick breath through your mouth, especially when you are surprised, shocked, or in pain.

big-time [bíg-tàim] a. 최고 수준의, 유명한; ad. 대단히; n. 대성공
If you describe a person as big-time, you mean they are successful and important.

producer [prədjú:sər] n. (영화·연극의) 제작자; 생산자, 생산 회사
A producer is a person whose job is to produce plays, films, programs, or CDs.

stare [stɛər] v. 빤히 쳐다보다, 응시하다; n. 빤히 쳐다보기, 응시
If you stare at someone or something, you look at them for a long time.

renew [rinjú:] v. 재개하다; 갱신하다; 새로 교체하다
If you renew an activity, you begin it again.

search [sə:rʧ] n. 찾기, 수색; v. 찾아보다, 뒤지다, 수색하다
A search is an attempt to find something or someone by looking for them carefully.

come by idiom 잠깐 들르다
If you come by somewhere, you visit a place for a short time, often when you are going somewhere else.

wonder [wʌ́ndər] v. 궁금해하다; (크게) 놀라다; n. 경탄, 경이
If you wonder about something, you think about it because it interests you and you want to know more about it.

cushion [kúʃən] n. 쿠션, 등받침; (두 개의 표면을 서로 분리해 주는) 층
A cushion is a fabric case filled with soft material, which you put on a seat to make it more comfortable.

spell [spel] v. (어떤 단어의) 철자를 말하다; 철자를 맞게 쓰다; n. 한동안, 잠깐; 주문, 마법
(spell out idiom 철자를 옳게 말하다; ~을 자세히 설명하다)
If you spell out a word, you say or write the letters of it in the correct order.

get the message idiom (힌트·암시 등의) 뜻을 알아채다
If you get the message, you understand what someone means, even if they do not say it directly.

loud and clear idiom 아주 이해하기 쉽게, 분명하게
If you tell someone something loud and clear, you are very easily understood, either because your voice is very clear or because you express yourself very clearly.

flip through idiom ~을 훑어보다, 휙휙 넘기다
If you flip through something such as a book, you turn over the pages of a book quickly without reading everything.

keep track of idiom ~에 대해 계속 알고 있다, ~을 놓치지 않다
If you keep track of a situation or a person, you make sure that you have the newest and most accurate information about them all the time.

lift [lift] v. 들어 올리다, 올리다; n. (들어)올리기; (차 등을) 태워 주기
If you lift something, you move it to another position, especially upward.

leave out of idiom ~에서 빼다
If you leave someone or something out of a certain matter, you do not involve them in it.

by the way idiom 그런데
You say 'by the way' when you add something to what you are saying, especially something that you have just thought of.

admit [ædmít] v. 인정하다, 시인하다
If you admit that something bad, unpleasant, or embarrassing is true, you agree, often unwillingly, that it is true.

scratch [skrætʃ] v. 긁다, 할퀴다; 긁히는 소리를 내다; n. 긁힌 자국; 긁히는 소리
If you scratch yourself, you rub your fingernails against your skin because it is itching.

freeze [fri:z] v. (froze-frozen) (두려움 등으로 몸이) 얼어붙다; 얼(리)다; n. 동결; 한파
If someone who is moving freezes, they suddenly stop and become completely still and quiet.

Chapter 8

1. How did Binky say he would feel about someone reading his diary?

A. He would feel bad and stop writing a diary after that.

B. He would feel like he was betrayed by his friends.

C. He didn't have a diary and wouldn't know how it felt.

D. He would feel embarrassed that someone knew his secrets.

2. How did Muffy want to decide who would read the diary?

A. She wanted them to play rock-paper-scissors.

B. She wanted them to spin the diary around like a compass.

C. She wanted to stand it on end and see where it fell.

D. She wanted to take turns reading in alphabetical order.

3. **Why did they stand the diary on end?**

    A. They thought that it might fall over and open by accident.

    B. They thought that they could see inside while it was standing.

    C. They thought that somebody might walk by and knock it over.

    D. They thought that it would fall and point to someone who had to read it.

4. **What did Muffy and Binky both do to try to open the diary?**

    A. They tried pushing it over.

    B. They tried kicking the table.

    C. They tried breathing on it.

    D. They tried waiting for an earthquake.

5. **What feeling would they all share equally if they read the diary?**

    A. They would all feel happy.

    B. They would all feel ashamed.

    C. They would all feel relieved.

    D. They would all feel guilty.

1분에 몇 단어를 읽는지 리딩 속도를 측정해보세요.

$$\frac{505 \text{ words}}{\text{reading time (} \qquad \text{) sec}} \times 60 = (\qquad) \text{ WPM}$$

Build Your Vocabulary

private [práivət] a. 사유의, 개인 소유의; 사적인; 은밀한; 혼자 있을 수 있는
Your private things belong only to you, or may only be used by you.

glare [glɛər] v. 노려보다; 눈부시다; n. 노려봄; 눈부심
If you glare at someone, you look at them with an angry expression on your face.

cover [kʌvər] n. (책이나 잡지의) 표지; 덮개; v. 씌우다, 가리다; 덮다
The cover of a book or a magazine is the outside part of it.

reach [riːʧ] v. (손·팔을) 뻗다, 내밀다; 이르다, 도달하다; n. 거리; 범위
If you reach somewhere, you move your arm and hand to take or touch something.

hesitate [hézətèit] v. 망설이다, 주저하다
If you hesitate, you do not speak or act for a short time, usually because you are uncertain, embarrassed, or worried about what you are going to say or do.

honest [ánist] a. (어떤 사실에 대해) 솔직한; 정직한 (honestly ad. 솔직히)
You use honestly to emphasize that you are referring to your, or someone else's, true beliefs or feelings.

settle [setl] v. 결정하다; 해결하다, 끝내다; (편하게) 앉다
If something is settled, it has all been decided and arranged.

✷ **definite** [défənit] a. 분명한, 뚜렷한; 확실한, 확고한 (definitely ad. 분명히, 틀림없이)
You use definitely to emphasize that something is the case, or to emphasize the strength of your intention or opinion.

✷ **spin** [spin] v. 돌리다, 회전시키다; (휙) 돌아서다; n. 회전, 돌기
If something spins or if you spin it, it turns quickly around a central point.

* **compass** [kʌ́mpəs] n. 나침반; (pl.) (제도용) 컴퍼스
A compass is an instrument that you use for finding directions. It has a dial and a magnetic needle that always points to the north.

복습 **point** [pɔint] v. (손가락 등으로) 가리키다; (길을) 알려 주다; n. 의미; 요점
If you point at a person or thing, you hold out your finger toward them in order to make someone notice them.

복습 **fair** [fɛər] a. 공정한; 아름다운; 타당한; n. 박람회
Something or someone that is fair is reasonable, right, and just.

✷✷ **accident** [ǽksidənt] n. 우연; 사고, 재해
If something happens by accident, it happens completely by chance.

* **upright** [ʌ́prait] a. 수직으로 세워 둔; (자세가) 똑바른, 꼿꼿한
If you put something upright, it is placed in a vertical position.

wobbly [wábli] a. (불안정하게) 흔들리는, 기우뚱한; 떨리는
Something that is wobbly moves unsteadily from side to side.

복습 **stare** [stɛər] v. 빤히 쳐다보다, 응시하다; n. 빤히 쳐다보기, 응시
If you stare at someone or something, you look at them for a long time.

복습 **blink** [bliŋk] v. 눈을 깜박이다; (불빛이) 깜박거리다; n. 눈을 깜박거림
When you blink or when you blink your eyes, you shut your eyes and very quickly open them again.

cross-eyed [krɔ́:s-àid] a. 사시(斜視)의
Someone who is cross-eyed has eyes that seem to look toward each other.

knock [nak] v. 치다; 부딪치다; (문을) 두드리다; n. 문 두드리는 소리; 부딪침

If you knock something, you touch or hit it roughly, especially so that it falls or moves.

flip [flip] v. 홱 뒤집다; 툭 던지다; n. 톡 던지기

If you flip through the pages of a book, for example, you quickly turn over the pages in order to find a particular one or to get an idea of the contents.

patient [péiʃənt] a. 참을성 있는; n. 환자 (patiently ad. 끈기 있게, 참을성 있게)

If you are patient, you stay calm and do not get annoyed.

come by idiom 잠깐 들르다

If you come by somewhere, you visit a place for a short time, often when you are going somewhere else.

blush [blʌʃ] v. 얼굴을 붉히다; ~에 부끄러워하다; n. 얼굴이 붉어짐

When you blush, your face becomes redder than usual because you are ashamed or embarrassed.

blow [blou] v. 입김을 내뿜다; (바람·입김에) 날리다; (악기 등을) 불다; n. 바람; 강타

If you blow, you send out a stream of air from your mouth.

silly [síli] a. 어리석은, 바보 같은; 유치한; n. 바보

If you say that someone or something is silly, you mean that they are foolish, childish, or ridiculous.

breathe [briːð] v. 호흡하다, 숨을 쉬다 (breathing n. 호흡)

When people or animals breathe, they take air into their lungs and let it out again.

exercise [éksərsaiz] n. 운동; 연습, 훈련; 활동; v. 운동하다; (권력·권리 등을) 행사하다

Exercises are a series of movements or actions which you do in order to get fit, remain healthy, or practice for a particular physical activity.

snort [snɔːrt] v. 코웃음을 치다, 콧방귀를 뀌다; n. 코웃음, 콧방귀

If someone snorts something, they say it in a way that shows contempt.

let out idiom (소리 등을) 내다, 지르다
To let out something means to suddenly make a loud sound such as a shout or cry.

breath [breθ] n. 숨, 입김
Your breath is the air that you let out through your mouth when you breathe.

sigh [sai] n. 한숨; 탄식; v. 한숨을 쉬다, 한숨짓다
A sigh is a long, deep audible exhalation expressing sadness, relief, or tiredness.

blame [bleim] v. ~을 탓하다, ~의 책임으로 보다; n. 책임; 탓
If you blame a person or thing for something bad, you believe or say that they are responsible for it or that they caused it.

cross [krɔ:s] v. 서로 겹치게 놓다; 가로지르다; 거스르다; n. 십자 기호; 십자가
If you cross your arms, legs, or fingers, you put one of them on top of the other.

huff and puff idiom (몹시 지쳐서) 헉헉거리다; (짜증이 나서) 씩씩대다
If you huff and puff, you breathe loudly, usually after physical exercise.

earthquake [ə́:rθkweik] n. 지진
An earthquake is a shaking of the ground caused by movement of the earth's crust.

cheat [ʧi:t] v. 부정행위를 하다, 속임수를 쓰다; 속이다; n. 속임수, 편법
(cheating n. 부정 행위)
When someone cheats, they do not obey a set of rules which they should be obeying, for example in a game or exam.

experiment [ikspérəmənt] n. 실험(적인 행동·방법); (과학적인) 실험;
v. (과학적인) 실험을 하다; 시험 삼아 해 보다
An experiment is the trying out of a new idea or method in order to see what it is like and what effects it has.

^{복습}**insist** [insíst] v. 고집하다, 주장하다, 우기다

If you insist that something is the case, you say so very firmly and refuse to say otherwise, even though other people do not believe you.

equal [íːkwəl] a. 동등한, 평등한; 동일한; v. 같다; 맞먹다 (equally ad. 똑같이, 동등하게)
Equally means to the same degree or extent.

guilty [gílti] a. 유죄의; 죄책감이 드는, 가책을 느끼는
If someone is guilty of doing something wrong, they have done that thing.

argue [áːrgjuː] v. 언쟁을 하다; 주장하다
If one person argues with another, they speak angrily to each other about something that they disagree about.

Chapter 9

1. **When did Sue Ellen start writing her diary?**

    A. The first day of first grade

    B. The first day she had a field trip

    C. The first day that she could write

    D. The first day that she moved to the city

2. **What did Ms. Turner say would happen if someone else found Sue Ellen's diary?**

    A. They would put it back on a shelf.

    B. They would turn it in at the desk.

    C. They would read it and spread her secrets.

    D. They would steal it and use it for their own diary.

3. **Why did Ms. Turner tell Sue Ellen that she had nothing to worry about?**

   A. She knew that Arthur had already found her diary.

   B. It had PRIVATE written on it where everyone could see it.

   C. Her staff would find her diary before any of the other students.

   D. Nobody was interested in reading diaries when they were busy with school work.

4. **Which of the following was NOT something that Sue Ellen's friends told her when they returned the diary to her?**

   A. They wanted to look inside.

   B. It was found on one of the carts.

   C. They were very sorry for reading it.

   D. Arthur was going to give it right back to her.

5. **What was Sue Ellen going to write about in her diary that night?**

   A. She would never bring her diary to school again.

   B. She could no longer trust her friends.

   C. She had lost her diary in the library.

   D. She had the best friends in the world.

1분에 몇 단어를 읽는지 리딩 속도를 측정해보세요.

$$\frac{478 \text{ words}}{\text{reading time } (\quad) \text{ sec}} \times 60 = (\qquad) \text{ WPM}$$

Build Your Vocabulary

복습 **staff** [stæf] n. 직원; v. 직원으로 일하다 (staff room n. 직원 사무실)
The staff of an organization are the people who work for it.

★ **console** [kənsóul] ① v. 위로하다, 위안을 주다 ② n. 콘솔, 제어반, 계기반
If you console someone who is unhappy about something, you try to make them feel more cheerful.

복습 **sigh** [sai] v. 한숨을 쉬다, 한숨짓다; n. 한숨; 탄식
When you sigh, you let out a deep breath, as a way of expressing feelings such as disappointment, tiredness, or pleasure.

after all idiom 어쨌든; 결국에는
You use after all when introducing a statement which supports or helps explain something you have just said.

turn up idiom 나타나다, 찾게 되다; 도착하다
If something that you have been looking for turns up, you find it unexpectedly.

★ **vanish** [vǽniʃ] v. 사라지다, 없어지다
If someone or something vanishes, they disappear suddenly or in a way that cannot be explained.

into thin air idiom 흔적도 없이
If someone or something disappears into thin air, they disappear completely.

nod [nad] v. (고개를) 끄덕이다, 끄덕여 나타내다; n. (고개를) 끄덕임

If you nod, you move your head downward and upward to show agreement, understanding, or approval.

stare [stɛər] v. 빤히 쳐다보다, 응시하다; n. 빤히 쳐다보기, 응시

If you stare at someone or something, you look at them for a long time.

dress up idiom (보통 때보다 더) 옷을 갖춰 입다

If you dress up, you put on clothes that are more formal than the clothes you usually wear.

bite [bait] v. (bit−bitten) (이빨로) 물다; n. 물기; 한 입

If you bite something, you use your teeth to cut into it, for example in order to eat it or break it.

rub [rʌb] v. (두 손 등을) 맞비비다, 문지르다; n. 문지르기, 비비기

If you rub two things together or if they rub together, they move backward and forward, pressing against each other.

be better off idiom (~하는 것이) 더 낫다

If you say that someone would be better off doing something, you are advising them to do it or expressing the opinion that it would benefit them to do it.

hunt [hʌnt] n. 수색, 추적; 사냥; v. (찾기 힘든 것을) 찾다; 사냥하다

Hunt is the activity of searching for a particular thing.

pat [pæt] v. 쓰다듬다, 토닥거리다; n. 쓰다듬기

If you pat something or someone, you tap them lightly, usually with your hand held flat.

turn in idiom ~을 돌려주다, 반납하다; ~을 제출하다

If you turn something in, you return it to the person it belongs to, especially something that was lost or was lent to you.

letter [létər] n. 글자, 문자; 편지; v. 글자가 들어 있다; 글자를 쓰다

Letters are written symbols which represent one of the sounds in a language.

admit [ædmít] v. 인정하다, 시인하다
If you admit that something bad, unpleasant, or embarrassing is true, you agree, often unwillingly, that it is true.

gasp [gæsp] v. 숨이 턱 막히다, 헉 하고 숨을 쉬다; n. 헉 하는 소리를 냄
When you gasp, you take a short quick breath through your mouth, especially when you are surprised, shocked, or in pain.

hug [hʌg] v. (무엇을) 끌어안다; 껴안다, 포옹하다; n. 껴안기, 포옹
If you hug something, you hold it close to your body with your arms tightly around it.

chest [ʧest] ① n. 가슴, 흉부 ② n. 상자, 궤
Your chest is the top part of the front of your body where your ribs, lungs, and heart are.

cart [kaːrt] n. 손수레, 카트; v. (수레나 차량으로) 운반하다; 손으로 들어 나르다
A cart is a shallow open container on wheels that may be pulled or pushed by hand.

cover [kʌ́vər] n. (책이나 잡지의) 표지; 덮개; v. 씌우다, 가리다; 덮다
The cover of a book or a magazine is the outside part of it.

tempt [tempt] v. 유혹하다, 부추기다; 유도하다
Something that tempts you attracts you and makes you want it, even though it may be wrong or harmful.

earthquake [ə́ːrθkweik] n. 지진
An earthquake is a shaking of the ground caused by movement of the earth's crust.

rule [ruːl] n. (개인적인) 원칙; (경기 등의) 규칙; 통치, 지배; 통치하다, 다스리다, 지배하다
Rules are instructions that tell you what you are allowed to do and what you are not allowed to do.

Chapter 10

1. What did Binky do as Sue Ellen was leaving the library?

   A. He held her books for her.

   B. He held open the door for her.

   C. He asked her to call him a gentleman.

   D. He held her hand as she walked down the stairs.

2. Why did Muffy tell Sue Ellen that she would be home tonight?

   A. Muffy could help her with any homework problems.

   B. Muffy could let her come over to play games.

   C. Muffy could give her ideas for stories.

   D. Muffy could just talk with her.

3. **What did Francine say was her best thing?**

   A. Being nice

   B. Being strong

   C. Being happy

   D. Being friendly

4. **Why did Sue Ellen say that Arthur might have been embarrassed if he had read her diary?**

   A. She had written down all of Arthur's flaws.

   B. She had drawn embarrassing pictures of Arthur.

   C. She had written some pretty nice things about Arthur.

   D. She had written down a lot of ways that Arthur could improve.

5. **Why did Arthur decide to write a diary of his own?**

   A. He wanted Sue Ellen to like him.

   B. He wanted to have his own secrets.

   C. He wanted to be popular like Sue Ellen.

   D. He wanted to practice his writing skills.

81

1분에 몇 단어를 읽는지 리딩 속도를 측정해보세요.

$$\frac{436 \text{ words}}{\text{reading time (} \quad \text{) sec}} \times 60 = (\quad) \text{ WPM}$$

Build Your Vocabulary

allow me idiom 제가 해 드리겠습니다
You can say 'allow me' when you are making a polite request or offering help.

deny [dinái] v. 부인하다, 부정하다; 거부하다
When you deny something, you state that it is not true.

rack [ræk] n. 받침대; 선반; v. 괴롭히다, 고통을 주다 (bike rack n. 자전거 보관대)
A rack is a frame or shelf, usually with bars or hooks, that is used for holding things or for hanging things on.

pedal [pedl] n. 페달; v. 페달을 밟다; (자전거를) 타고 가다
The pedals on a bicycle are the two parts that you push with your feet in order to make the bicycle move.

by the way idiom 그런데
You say 'by the way' when you add something to what you are saying, especially something that you have just thought of.

resourceful [risɔ́:rsfəl] a. 임기응변의 재주가 있는, 재치 있는
Someone who is resourceful is good at finding ways of dealing with problems.

come up idiom 생기다, 발생하다; 언급되다
If something comes up, it happens, especially when you do not expect it.

복습 **nod** [nad] v. (고개를) 끄덕이다, 끄덕여 나타내다; n. (고개를) 끄덕임
If you nod, you move your head downward and upward to show agreement, understanding, or approval.

ride [raid] v. (rode–ridden) (말·자전거·오토바이 등을) 타다;
n. (차량·자전거 등을) 타고 달리기; 여정
When you ride a bicycle or a motorcycle, you sit on it, control it, and travel along on it.

lock [lak] v. (자물쇠로) 잠그다; 고정시키다; n. 자물쇠 (unlock v. (열쇠로) 열다)
If you unlock something such as a door, a room, or a container that has a lock, you open it using a key.

friendly [fréndli] a. 친절한, 우호적인
If someone is friendly, they behave in a pleasant, kind way, and like to be with other people.

considerate [kənsídərət] a. 사려 깊은, (남을) 배려하는
Someone who is considerate pays attention to the needs, wishes, or feelings of other people.

mention [ménʃən] v. 말하다, 언급하다; n. 언급, 거론
If you mention something, you say something about it, usually briefly.

복습 **confuse** [kənfjúːz] v. (사람을) 혼란시키다; 혼동하다 (confused a. 혼란스러워 하는)
If you are confused, you do not know exactly what is happening or what to do.

복습 **expect** [ikspékt] v. 예상하다, 기대하다; 요구하다
If you expect something to happen, you believe that it will happen.

복습 **private** [práivət] a. 은밀한; 사유의, 개인 소유의; 사적인; 혼자 있을 수 있는
Your private thoughts or feelings are ones that you do not talk about to other people.

복습 **pause** [pɔːz] v. (말·일을 하다가) 잠시 멈추다; 정지시키다; n. 멈춤
If you pause while you are doing something, you stop for a short period and then continue.

복습 criticism [krítəsìzm] n. (좋지 못한 점을 지적하는) 비판, 비난; 비평, 평론
Criticism is the action of expressing disapproval of something or someone.

복습 improve [imprúːv] v. 개선되다, 나아지다; 향상시키다
If something improves or if you improve it, it gets better.

복습 hold back idiom ~을 비밀로 하다, 말하지 않다; (감정을) 누르다; 방해하다
if you hold back something, you stop yourself from expressing or showing how you feel.

positive [pázətiv] a. 확신하는; 긍정적인; 분명한, 결정적인; n. 긍정적인 것
If you are positive about something, you are completely sure about it.

embarrass [imbǽrəs] v. 당황스럽게 하다, 쑥스럽게 하다; 곤란하게 하다
(embarrassed a. 쑥스러운, 당황스러운)
A person who is embarrassed feels shy, ashamed, or guilty about something.

복습 blink [bliŋk] v. 눈을 깜박이다; (불빛이) 깜박거리다; n. 눈을 깜박거림
When you blink or when you blink your eyes, you shut your eyes and very quickly open them again.

복습 suppose [səpóuz] v. (~이라고) 생각하다, 추측하다; 가정하다
If you suppose that something is true, you believe that it is probably true, because of other things that you know.

puzzle [pʌzl] v. 어리둥절하게 하다; n. 퍼즐; 수수께끼 (puzzled a. 어리둥절해하는)
Someone who is puzzled is confused because they do not understand something.

복습 blush [blʌʃ] v. 얼굴을 붉히다; ~에 부끄러워하다; n. 얼굴이 붉어짐
When you blush, your face becomes redder than usual because you are ashamed or embarrassed.

seal [siːl] v. 봉인하다; 확정 짓다, 다짐하다; n. 직인, 도장; [동물] 바다표범
(sealed a. 봉인된)
You can use 'my lips are sealed' for saying that you will not tell a secret to anyone else.

frown [fraun] v. 얼굴을 찌푸리다; n. 찡그림, 찌푸림

When someone frowns, their eyebrows become drawn together, because they are annoyed or puzzled.

fair [fɛər] a. 공정한; 타당한; 아름다운; n. 박람회

Something or someone that is fair is reasonable, right, and just.

in that case idiom 그런 경우에는, 그렇다면

You say 'in that case' to indicate that what you are going to say is true if the possible situation that has just been mentioned actually exists.

screech [skri:ʃ] v. (차량 등이) 끼익 하는 소리를 내다; n. 끼익 (하는 날카로운 소리)

If a vehicle screeches somewhere or if its tires screech, its tires make an unpleasant high-pitched noise on the road.

put in idiom (편지·이야기 등의 속에) ～을 집어넣다; (남이 말하는데) 끼어들다

If you put something in a story or letter, you include them in it.

page 7

도서관의 바쁜 오후였습니다. 많은 사람들이 돌아다니면서, 책을 고르거나 조사를 하고 있었습니다.

한 탁자에, 수 엘렌이 혼자 앉아 있었습니다. 그녀는 누가 지나가도 올려다보지 않았고, 지나가는 대화에도 관심을 기울이지 않았습니다. 그녀는 자신의 일기장에 글을 쓰는 것에 집중하고 있었습니다.

일기장에게. 오늘 도서관은 붐비는 곳이야. 많은 내 친구들이 여기에서 학교 과제를 하고 있어. 내게 이렇게 많고 다양한 친구들이 있다는 것이 재미있다고 난 가끔 생각해. 나는 가끔씩 왜 내가 그들과 친구가 되었고 다른 사람들과는 되지 않았는지 궁금해.

page 8

내가 만약 새 친구들을 사귈 수 있다면, 나는 어떤 사람들을 원할까? 늘 나에게 선물을 주거나 자원해서 내 방을 청소해주는 친구들일까? 아니면 어쩌면 나는 TV 프로그램이나 영화에 출연하는 유명한 친구들을 좋아할 수도 있겠지. 그런데, 누군가를 진정한 친구로 만들어 주는 것은 무엇일까?

수 엘렌은 자신의 펜을 내려놓았습니다. 지금은 그것으로 충분했습니다. 그

녀는 자신의 은밀한 생각들을 적을 수 있는 특별한 공간인 일기장을 갖고 있다는 사실이 좋았습니다. 그녀의 생각들이 언제나 멋지거나 중요한 것인 아니었습니다. 하지만 그녀는 종이에, 자신이 볼 수 있는 곳에 글을 쓰는 것이 좋았습니다.

그녀는 일기장을 덮었고 손가락으로 제본의 가장자리를 훑었습니다. 수 엘렌은 직접 그 표지를 디자인했습니다. 그녀는 반짝이가 든 펜으로 *나의 일기장*이라고 깔끔하게 써 넣었습니다. 그 아래에, 그녀는 큰 글씨로 **개인적인 것** 그리고 **열어보지 마시오**라고 덧붙였습니다.

page 9

도서관 시계가 네 번 울리며, 수 엘렌에게 이제 가야 할 시간인 것을 알려주었습니다. 그녀는 대출하고 싶은 책들을 모두 집어 들었고 그것들을 그녀의 학교 공책과 일기장 위에 쌓았습니다. 그녀는 자기 팔 안에 모든 것을 끼워 넣고서 대출대로 걸어갔습니다. 그녀는 균형을 잡기 위해 팔을 움직여야 했고, 그녀가 그렇게 했을 때, 그녀의 일기장이 그 더미에서 미끄러지며 빠졌고 카펫 위로 조용히 떨어졌습니다.

터너 선생님은 대출대에 앉아서, 책과 관련해서 사람들을 도우려고 기다리고 있었습니다. 그녀는 수 엘렌을 보고는 미소 지었습니다.

"그건 참 인상적인 더미네. 이번 주에 네가 책을 아주 많이 읽을 거라는 걸 알겠구나."

"저는 결정할 수가 없었어요." 수 엘렌이 인정했습니다. "선택할 수 있는 좋은 책들이 너무 많았어요."

터너 선생님이 책들은 대출하기 시작하자, 수 엘렌은 대출대 위에 그것들을 펼쳤습니다.

page 10

그녀가 마지막 책에 다다랐을 때, 그녀는 그 아래에 자신의 일기장이 보일 것이라고 생각했습니다.

하지만 그녀가 본 모두는 자신의 공책이었습니다.

곧바로, 그녀는 다른 책들 사이를 뒤졌습니다.

"뭐 잘못된 거 있니?" 터너 선생님이 물었습니다.

"아니요, 그런 것 같지는 않은데... 사실, 네." 수 엘렌이 바닥을 둘러보았습니다. 그녀에게 보이는 것이라고는 오직 종이 클립 두 개와 지우개뿐이었습니다.

"저 뭔가를 잃어버린 것 같아요!" 그녀가 말했습니다.

재빨리, 그녀는 자신이 앉아 있었던 탁자 쪽으로 왔던 길을 되짚어갔습니다. 일기장은 그곳에 없었습니다. 그것은 어디로 사라져 버린 것일까요? 일기장은 마법처럼 없어지지 않습니다. 그

리고 그것들은 스스로 걸어가 버리지도 않습니다.

그녀는 무릎을 꿇고 의자와 탁자 밑을 살펴보면서, 필요한 경우에는 다른 사람들의 발을 옆으로 밀쳤습니다.

"잠깐만요. 악! 내 손가락 좀 조심하세요. 지나갈게요."

수 엘렌은 그녀가 걸어갔던 것을 기억하는 모든 곳을 뒤졌고—그녀가 가지 않았던 몇몇 장소도 뒤졌습니다. 그녀는 심지어 휴지통도 뒤졌습니다.

page 12

하지만 소용없었습니다. 일기장은 어디에도 보이지 않았습니다.

2장

page 13

수 엘렌은 간신히 대출대로 돌아왔습니다. 그녀의 얼굴을 붉었고, 그녀의 눈가는 촉촉했습니다.

"무슨 일 있니?" 수 엘렌이 속상하다는 걸 보게 된, 터너 선생님이 물었습니다.

"제 일기장을 잃어버렸어요. 제가 방금 전까지 갖고 있었거든요. 저는 이해할 수가 없어요. 저는 분명히 여기에 두고 갔을 거예요." 그녀는 책상을 다시 훑어보았습니다. "하지만 그런 것 같지

않네요.”

“내 도서관 안에서는 책이 사라지지 않는단다.” 터너 선생님이 그녀에게 장담했습니다. “나에게 그것을 묘사해 보렴.”

수 엘렌은 숨을 깊게 들이마셨습니다. “음, 그건 책처럼 생겼어요. 반짝거리는 빨간 가죽 표지가 있고요. 뭐, 적어도 그건 가죽처럼 보여요. 그리고 파란색 반짝이 글자로 **내 일기장**이라고 쓰여 있어요. 그리고 그 밑에 저는 **개인적인 것. 열어보지 마시오**라고 써놓았어요.”

page 14

“아주 구체적이구나.” 터너 선생님이 말했습니다. “그게 우리가 찾는 걸 더 쉽게 해줄 거야. 걱정하지 마—우리는 찾을 수 있을 거야. 내가 직원 모두에게 세심하게 살펴보라고 말할게.”

“고마워요. 저도 직접 계속 찾아봐야 할 것 같아요. 제가 그저 바라는 것은...”

수 엘렌은 그녀가 어떤 웃음소리를 들었기 때문에 잠시 말을 멈추었습니다. 그것은 여자아이가 비밀 일기장을 보고 있다면 정확히 낼 법한 소리였습니다.

“다시 돌아올게요.” 그녀가 터너 선생님에게 말했습니다.

수 엘렌은 소리가 들려오는 곳을 따라서 구석으로 갔고, 그곳에는 프랜신이 책 위로 몸을 숙이고 있었습니다.

“일기장이 저기로 사라졌던 것이구나!” 수 엘렌이 말했습니다.

그녀는 단호하게 책상으로 걸어갔습니다.

“참 재미있지, 응, 프랜신?”

프랜신이 고개를 끄덕였습니다. “그러니까 말이야. 이것 좀 들어봐—”

page 15

“난 그걸 들을 필요가 없어.” 수 엘렌이 말했습니다. “내가 그걸 썼다고!” 그녀가 프랜신에게서 책을 확 낚아챘습니다. “이봐!”

“그리고 다른 사람의 일기장을 훔치는 건 하나도 재미있지 않아. 난 너한테 놀랐어, 프랜신. 난 네가 나의—” 수 엘렌은 책을 내려다보았습니다. 그것은 빨간색이었지만, 파란색의 반짝이 글자는 없었습니다. “어, 이건 내 일기장이 아니잖아.”

“당연히 아니지.” 프랜신이 말했습니다. “이건 유머 책이라고. 내가 네 일기장을 가지고 뭘 하겠니?”

“몰라. 네가 주웠을 수도 있잖아. 그건 빨간색이고 **개인적인 것**이라고 위에 적혀있어. 나는 방금 전에는 갖고 있었는데, 이제 그건 없어졌어.”

“참 이상하네.” 프랜신이 말했습니다. “넌 그걸 도둑맞았다고 생각하니?

수 엘렌은 어떻게 생각해야 할지 알 수 없었습니다. “그건 나한테만 소중해.

나는 계속 거기에 글을 써 왔어."

"난 일기장을 가져본 적이 없어." 프랜신이 말했습니다. "거기에다가 뭘 쓰는 거니?"

page 16

"내 생각, 하루 동안 일어났던 일. 은밀한 생각들. 그걸 찾는 건 나에게 몹시 중요해, 프랜신. 그러니까, 거기에는 모든 사람에 대한 것들이 쓰여 있단 말이야."

프랜신의 눈이 크게 커졌습니다. "모든 사람이라고? 네가 모든 사람이라고 한 건, 그러니까 정말 모두라는 뜻이야?"

"그래, 그래, 하지만 그건 지금 중요한 게 아니야."

"나한테는 중요해." 프랜신이 말했습니다. "넌 뭐라고 썼는데?"

"난 지금 그것에 대해서 말할 수 없어. 나는 내 일기장을 찾아야만 해."

프랜신이 더 말하기도 전에, 수 엘렌은 급히 가 버렸습니다. 빨리 일기장을 찾지 못한다면, 그녀는 자신이 무슨 짓을 할지 몰랐습니다.

3장

page 18

"수 엘렌에게 무슨 문제 있니?" 머피가 프랜신에게 물었습니다.

"그녀는 일기장을 잃어버려서 아주 속상해하고 있어. 그것은 앞에 **개인적인 것**이라고 쓰여 있어. 그녀는 심지어 내가 읽고 있었다고 생각했다고." 프랜신은 고개를 저었습니다. "난 그게 왜 그녀를 속상하게 하는지 모르겠어."

"흐으으음." 머피가 말했습니다. "아마도 그녀가 너에 대해서 뭔가를 써 놓았나 보지—뭔가 네가 읽지 않았으면 하는 것 말이야."

"나에 대한 거라고?" 프랜신은 자신의 허리에 손을 짚었습니다. "하지만 그녀가 나에 대해 뭐라고 썼겠어?"

"아마도 네가 그녀에게 한 모든 못된 일에 대해 썼겠지."

page 19

프랜신은 놀란 것처럼 보였습니다. "무슨 일?"

머피는 팔짱을 꼈습니다. "어제 그녀를 진흙탕으로 밀었던 것과 같은 일말이야."

"나는 그녀를 밀지 않았어." 프랜신이 주장했습니다. "그녀가 발을 헛디딘 거지."

"하지만, 네 바로 옆에서 그랬지."

"난 그냥 어쩌다 보니 거기 있었던 거야. 난 진흙탕으로 사람을 밀지 않아."

"글쎄, 넌 웃었잖아."

"물론, 난 웃었지. 그건 웃겼다고. 그

녀는 진흙을 뒤집어썼잖아."

　머피는 팔짱을 꼈습니다. "너는 그녀가 넘어졌을 때 그녀 바로 옆에 서 있었고, 그 다음에 너는 웃었어. 만약에 그녀가 네가 자기를 밀었다고 생각한다면 어떡하니?"

　프랜신은 입술을 깨물었습니다.

　그녀는 갑자기 하얀 가운을 입은 수염이 난 의사가 커다란 책상 뒤에 앉아 있는 것을 보았습니다. 문을 두드리는 소리가 난 뒤, 수 엘렌이 들어왔습니다. 그녀에게 진흙이 잔뜩 튀어 있었습니다.

page 20

　"예약을 했나요?" 의사가 물었습니다.

　"아니요." 수 엘렌이 인정했습니다. "하지만 저는 선생님을 바로 만나야만 했어요, 지머 박사님. 이건 긴급 상황이에요."

　"아! 어떤 유형의 긴급 상황이죠?"

　수 엘렌이 자신의 팔을 내밀었습니다. "모르시겠어요? 프랜신이 방금 저를 진흙으로 밀었다고요."

　의사는 자기 수염을 쓰다듬었습니다. "그렇군요." 그가 말했습니다.

　수 엘렌은 자신의 일기장을 찾아보았습니다. "그것은 이번 달에 프랜신이 저에게 못되게 굴었던 열일곱 번째 일이에요. 뭔가 조치를 취해야 해요! 제가 선생님을 찾아온 것은 선생님이 못된 아이들에 대한 세계 최고의 전문가이기

때문이에요."

　"맞아요, 맞아." 의사가 말했습니다. "제가 그걸 좀 봐도 될까요?" 그가 수 엘렌에게서 일기장을 받아 빠르게 훑어보았습니다.

　"아, 그래요." 그가 말했습니다. "밀기. 웃기. 당신의 간식 파이에서 과일 속만 먹고 당신에게는 딱딱한 껍질만 남기기." 그가 한숨을 쉬었습니다. "유감스럽지만 당신의 친구는 심한 괴물병의 모든 증세를 보이고 있어요."

page 21

　"괴물병이요?"

　"맞아요." 의사는 그의 책상 위에 있는 단추를 눌렀고, 반짝거리는 TV 화면이 벽에 나타났습니다. 그것은 다른 아이들에게 소리 지르는 한 여자아이를 보여줬습니다. 그때 그녀가 그들 가운데 한 명을 밀었습니다.

　"보시다시피." 의사가 계속 말했습니다. "이것은 환자가 그녀의 못된 짓을 절제하지 못하는 질병입니다."

　"저건 프랜신이에요!"

　지머 박사가 영상을 정지시켰습니다. "우리는 그녀를 오랜 시간 동안 지켜봤습니다. 그녀를 도울 방도가 없는 것이 유감입니다. 우리는 반드시 그녀를 다른 어린이들로부터 떨어뜨려놔야 합니다!"

　바로 그 순간 프랜신이 그들에게 들

이닥쳤습니다. 그녀는 수 엘렌을 손가락으로 가리켰습니다. "나는 내가 너를 여기서 찾을 줄 알았어!"

하지만 프랜신이 뭔가를 더 해 보기도 전에, 유니폼을 입은 경비원 두 명이 뛰어 들어왔고 그녀를 붙잡았습니다.

page 23

"나를 내버려 둬!" 프랜신이 소리쳤습니다.

"미안해." 경비원들 중 한 명이 말했습니다. "하지만 괴물병은 아주 전염성이 심해. 우리는 너를 당장 내쫓아야 해."

"게다가." 두 번째 경비원이 말했습니다. "다른 아이들은 너와 놀고 싶어 하지 않아. 너는 그들에게 너무 못되게 굴었어."

"하지만 전 바뀔 수 있어요! 정말이에요!"

경비원들이 웃었습니다.

"만약에 우리가 그 말을 들을 때마다 5센트 동전을 받았다면…," 첫 번째 경비원이 말했습니다.

"우리는 아마 엄청 많은 5센트 동전을 갖고 있겠지." 그 두 번째 경비원이 문장을 마쳤습니다.

그리고는 그들 둘 다 다시 웃었습니다.

page 24

"하지만 저에게 한 번 더 기회를 줘야 해요." 프랜신이 말했습니다. "나는 괴물병이 없어요."

"너한테 뭐가 없다고?" 머피가 물었습니다.

프랜신은 눈을 깜빡였습니다. 그녀는 다시 도서관에 있었습니다.

"그건 질병이야. 수 엘렌이 아마 자신의 일기장에 써 놓았을지도 몰라."

프랜신이 일어나서 자기 이마를 닦았습니다. "난 마실 게 필요해."

그녀는 급수대로 향했습니다.

"프랜신은 가끔 너무 흥분을 잘 해." 머피가 혼잣말을 했습니다. "수 엘렌은 아마 전혀 그녀에 대해서 쓰지 않았을 거야." 그녀가 말을 멈추면서, 선반에 기대었습니다. "물론, 그녀는 무언가에 대해서 써야만 했을 거야. 하지만, 매일 일어나는 일은 엄청 지루할 수 있어. 그녀는 아마도 이야기를 지어내야만 했을 거야.…"

page 25

머피는 긴 거울을 들여다보고 있는 자신의 모습을 보았습니다. 그녀는 길게 늘어진 드레스를 입고 머리에는 보석이 박힌 왕관을 쓰고 공주처럼 옷을 입고 있었습니다.

수 엘렌은 그녀 옆에 서 있었습니다. 그녀는 보석이 없는 평범한 드레스를 입고 있었습니다.

"밀리센타 공주님." 수 엘렌이 말했습니다. "누구도 당신과 견줄 수 없어요."

"계속 말하렴." 머피가 말했습니다.

"당신은 부유하지요."

"맞아."

"당신은 아름다워요."

"그 또한 맞아."

"그리고 당신은 이 땅에서 가장 똑똑한 공주예요."

"세 가지 다 맞아." 머피가 동의했습니다.

"당신은 정말 예뻐요." 수 엘렌이 계속 말했습니다. "반면에 저는 그냥 평범하고요."

그림자가 잠시 태양을 가렸습니다.

"누가 감히 내 좋은 날씨를 방해하는 거지?" 머피가 물었습니다.

수 엘렌은 창 밖을 내다보았고 헉 하고 숨을 뱉었습니다. "용이에요!" 그녀가 외쳤습니다. "불을 내뿜는 용이에요. 그리고 그것이 마을에 큰 문제를 일으키고 있어요."

머피가 자신의 머리카락을 빗었습니다. "마을 사람들은 어떻게 대처하고 있지?"

"그들은 이쪽으로 도망치고 있어요!"

"그들이?" 공주는 놀랐습니다.

"도와주세요!" 마을 사람들이 외쳤습니다. "도와주세요, 부유하고 아름답고 똑똑한 밀리센타 공주님!"

머피가 한숨 쉬었습니다. "우리가 무언가를 해야 할 것 같은데."

"두려워하지 마세요, 공주님!" 수 엘렌이 갑옷을 입으며, 말했습니다. "제가 처리할게요!"

그녀가 철커덕거리며 탑의 계단을 내려가기 시작했지만, 잠시 뒤에, 철커덕거리는 소리가 멈췄습니다.

"무슨 일이야?" 머피가 물었습니다. "넌 왜 멈춘 거니?"

"으윽." 수 엘렌이 외쳤습니다. "저 문가에 끼었어요." 그녀가 헉 하고 숨을 쉬었습니다. "그리고 용이 다가오고 있어요!"

머피가 창 밖을 내다보았습니다. 용이 언덕을 올라오고 있었습니다.

머피는 한숨 쉬었습니다. "만약 뭔가 제대로 되길 바란다면, 네 스스로 해야만 하지." 그녀는 자신의 길고, 땋은 머리카락의 끝을 잡았고 그것을 창 밖의 임시 도르래에 꿰었습니다. 그리고 그녀는 자신의 몸을 땅으로 내렸습니다.

용이 수 엘렌을 바싹 구울 준비를 하고 있을 때, 머피가 자신의 향수 한 병을 그것에게 뿌렸습니다.

용의 불이 꺼졌습니다.

"오, 공주님!" 수 엘렌이 칭찬을 마구 쏟아냈습니다. "정말 감사해요! 저는 이 은혜를 어떻게 갚을지 모르겠네요!"

"음, 이 향수는 한 병에 *30달러*거든. 거기서부터 시작하면 되겠어."

수 엘렌이 한숨을 쉬었습니다. "공주님은 분명히 세상에서 가장 현실적인 공주일거예요."

"맞아." 머피가 행복하게 말했습니다. "나도 그런 것 같아."

5장

page 29

"이봐, 이 멍한 녀석아!" 빙키가 말하며, 머피의 어깨를 두드렸습니다.

머피는 눈을 깜빡였습니다. "그게 뭐야? 넌 나에게 그런 식으로 말해서는 안 돼. 나는 공주라고."

빙키는 그저 어깨를 으쓱 올렸습니다. "좋아, 좋아. 하지만 네가 무엇이건 간에, 네가 선반을 막고 있다고. 나는 저기 뒤에 있는 책을 봐야 해."

"오, 미안해." 머피가 옆으로 비켜섰습니다. "난 수 엘렌의 일기장에 대해서 생각하고 있었던 것 같아. 그녀는 그것을 잃어버렸거든."

page 30

"운이 나쁘네."

"거기에는 나에 대한 멋진 이야기가 담겨 있지...."

빙키는 혼란스러워 보였습니다. "난 그게 수 엘렌의 일기장인 줄 알았는데."

"뭐, 맞아. 하지만 일기장은 네 친구들에 대해 쓰기에 좋은 곳이지."

"정말?" 빙키가 말했습니다. "이 일기장이 어떻게 생겼는데?"

"나도 잘 몰라. 하지만 거기에는 **개인적인 것**이라고 적혀 있어."

"나 그런 책을 봤어." 빙키가 말했습니다. "그건 바닥에 있었어. 난 수레들 가운데 하나에 그걸 올려놨지."

"그랬어?"

빙키는 고개를 끄덕였습니다. "바닥에 책을 두는 건 좋지 않잖아."

"너 그 안을 봤니?" 머피가 물었습니다.

"아니." 빙키가 말했습니다. "내가 왜 그러겠어? 내가 쓰고 있는 보고서는 **개인적인 것**과 그 어떤 상관도 없는걸."

"알아, 나도 안다고." 머피가 말했습니다. "하지만 그게 중요한 게 아니야. 일기장은 아주, 음, 흥미로울 수 있다는 거지. 사람들은 그들이 모든 것에 대해 진짜로 어떻게 느끼는지 적어놓으니까."

page 31

"모든 것이라고?"

머피가 고개를 끄덕였습니다. "그리고 모든 사람들에 대해서. 난 그저 우리가 그걸 찾을 수 있으면 좋겠어."

그녀는 찾는 일을 도울 수 있을지 확인하려고 떠났습니다.

빙키는 감명을 받았습니다. "모든 사람들이란 말이지, 흠?" 그가 혼잣말을 했습니다. 일기장을 갖는 것은 힘든 일처럼 들렸습니다. 일기장을 쓰는 것은 그에게 그다지 매력적이지 않았습니다. 하지만 만약 수 엘렌이 모든 사람들에 대하여 쓰고 있었다면…

빙키는 책을 집으려고 손을 뻗었지만, 그의 팔은 허공에서 얼어붙었습니다.

"그건 심지어 나도 포함되는 거잖아!" 그가 깨달았습니다.

빙키는 수 엘렌이 자신의 침실 안의 책상 앞에 앉아있는 것을 보았습니다. 그녀는 자신의 일기장에 적고 있었습니다.

일기장에게: 오늘은 아주 특별했어. 나는 오늘 내 이상형의 남자인, 빙키 반스와 내 대부분의 시간을 함께 보낼 수 있었어.

page 33

그녀는 여백에 빙키의 그림을 그렸습니다. 그는 마치 영화배우처럼 선글라스를 쓰고 있었습니다.

그는 매우 잘생겼고—또한, 강해. 오늘 학

교 버스가 진흙탕에 빠졌는데, 빙키는 버스의 뒷부분을 들어 올리겠다고 자원했어. 버스 운전사는 그럴 필요 없다고 말했어. 하지만 빙키는 어쨌든 그렇게 했고, 운전사는 신경 쓰는 것 같지 않았어.

나는 다른 남자아이들이 모두 빙키를 우러러보는 것을 알 수 있어. 누가 그들을 비난할 수 있겠어? 난 단지 빙키가 나를 알아봐 주기를 바랄 뿐이야. 나는 그에게 많이 미소 지으려고 하지만, 그는 그저 내 얼굴이 왜 그러냐고 물을 뿐이야. 나는 운동장에서 그를 쫓아다니지만, 그는 내가 길을 잃기라도 했는지 알고 싶어 하지. 나는 심지어 점심시간에 그에게 별도의 디저트를 가져다 주기 시작했어. 적어도 그것은 그의 관심을 끌었지. 그리고 나는 그가 디저트를 좋아한다는 것을 알아. 왜냐하면 그는 먹은 후에 늘 트림하거든.

하지만, 난 내가 그에게 내가 어떻게 느끼는지 말하지 않은 채, 계속 이럴 수 있는지 잘 모르겠어. 아마도 오늘 밤 나는 그의 집으로 가서 그의 창문 아래에서 세레나데라도 불러야 할 것 같아. 만약 그것이 그에게 내 마음을 보여주지 못한다면, 그 무엇도 할 수 없을 거야.

6장

page 35

"무슨 일이야, 빙키?" 아서가 말했습니

다. "넌 마치 자유의 여신상 같아 보여."

"응?" 빙키가 그의 팔을 돌처럼 떨어뜨렸습니다.

아서는 그가 고른 책더미를 잔뜩 들고 있었습니다. "너 괜찮은 거야? 너 조금 이상하게 보여."

"아니, 아니야, 난 괜찮아. 잊지 마, 내가 버스의 뒷부분을 들 수 있다는 것을."

"네가 뭘 할 수 있다고?"

"음, 신경 쓰지 마." 빙키는 화제를 바꾸고 싶었습니다. "너 들었어? 수 엘렌이 그녀의 일기장을 잃어버렸대. 나는 그걸 수레에 놓았어."

아서는 인상을 찡그렸습니다. "넌 왜 그녀에게 그걸 돌려주지 않았어?"

"난 그때 그게 그녀의 일기장인지 몰랐어. 그건 그냥 앞에 개인적인 것이라고 적혀있는 책일 뿐이었거든."

"개인적인 것이라고?" 아서가 말했습니다. "왜 그런지 궁금하네."

빙키가 몸서리를 쳤습니다. "너는 네가 원하는 만큼 궁금해할 수 있지만, 내게서 어떤 도움도 바라지는 마. 난 궁금해하는 건 끝냈어. 나중에 보자."

"잘 가." 아서가 말했습니다. 그는 빙키가 약간 이상하게 행동하고 있다고 생각했습니다. 아마도 팔을 그렇게 올리고 있었던 것이 그의 뇌로 가는 혈액

공급을 방해한 것인지도 몰랐습니다.

수 엘렌의 일기장에 대한 일은 정말 안 됐습니다. 아서는 사람들이 자신이 생각하는 모든 것을 늘 공개적으로 이야기하지 않는다는 것을 알았습니다. 하지만 그녀의 일기장 속에서는, 특히 개인적인 것이라고 하는 모든 상황을 봤을 때, 수 엘렌은 아마도 망설이지 않을 것입니다.

"아서, 너 저 책들 전부를 갖고 뭐 하려는 거니?"

"뭘 하다니?" 아서가 말했습니다. "난 그것들을 대출하려고 하고 있지."

수 엘렌이 제목들을 훑어보았습니다. "미라의 저주에 대한 비밀, 화성의 괴상한 운하. 아서, 난 네가 이런 걸 읽는다니 믿을 수 없어."

"왜 안 돼?"

"이건 네게 좋지 않아. 너 악몽을 꾸지 않니?"

"책 읽는 것 때문에 꾸진 않아." 아서가 말했습니다. "난 모험을 좋아한다고."

"오, 그래? 너 지난주에 악몽 꾼 적은 없니?"

"그—그런 것 같은데."

수 엘렌은 팔짱을 꼈습니다. "그리고 지난주에 이런 종류의 책들을 읽은 적 있니?"

"뭐, 그랬지..."

"내 말이 맞잖아." 수 엘렌이 말했습니다. "있잖아, 아서, 난 너를 아주 자세히 지켜보고 있었어."

"네가 그랬다고?"

수 엘렌이 고개를 끄덕였습니다. "넌 완벽하지 않아, 아서. 사실, 넌 개선할 것들이 많지. 난 내 일기장에 너의 결점들을 모두 기록하고 있었어."

"네가 그 모든 귀찮은 일들을 하지 않아도 됐을 텐데." 아서가 말했습니다.

"오, 그건 하나도 어렵지 않았어." 수 엘렌이 말했습니다. "나는 계속 내 일기장에 모든 것을 정리해 놓았지. 하지만 난 더 이상 그냥 이런 것들을 쓰기만 할 수는 없어. 난 행동을 취해야만 하지."

"어떤 행동?"

"너 같은 사람들을 개선시키는 것 말이야. 난 네가 바뀔 수 있는 방법에 대한 목록을 만들었어."

그녀는 자신의 주머니에서 종이 두루마리를 꺼냈습니다. 그것은 그녀의 발로 떨어지고 풀어져서 방의 절반을 가로질러 갔습니다.

"'1번.'" 그녀가 크게 읽었습니다.

아서는 한숨 쉬었습니다. 그는 빠져나갈 방법을 찾아 주위를 둘러보았습니다.

수 엘렌은 읽기를 멈추었습니다. "난 그 표정을 알아. 아마 우리는 바로 78번으로 넘어가야 할 것 같아."

아서는 물어보기가 거의 두려웠습니다. "그게 뭔데?" 그가 마침내 말했습니다.

수 엘렌은 종이를 따라 이동했습니다. "'78번: 비판을 잘 수용하지 않는다.' 이제, 가만히 앉아 있을래? 우리는 해야 할 일이 있다고."

빠져나갈 수 있는 방법은 없는 것 같았습니다. 하지만 수 엘렌이 목록의 맨 위에 있는 것을 찾아가면서, 그녀는 한쪽으로 살짝 움직였습니다. 아서는 기회를 보았습니다—그리고 책꽂이들 사이에 난 틈으로 급히 움직였습니다.

7장

"이봐! 조심해!" 아서가 그의 수레를 부딪칠 때 도서관 조수 한 명이 외쳤습니다.

책들이 날아가 버렸습니다.

"죄송합니다." 아서가 말하며, 바닥에서 자신의 몸을 일으켰습니다. "제가 뭘 하려고 했냐면... 음, 아무것도 아니에요."

"이 난장판 좀 봐." 그 조수가 말했습

니다. 그는 책들을 줍기 시작했습니다.

"여기, 제가 도와드릴게요." 아서가 말했습니다.

조수는 펄쩍 뛰며 뒤로 물러섰습니다. "네가 다시 나에게 달려들지 않을 거라는 걸 내가 어떻게 아니?"

"전 당신에게 달려든 것이 아니었어요." 아서가 말했습니다. "나는 그저 도망가려고 했던 거예요."

page42

"도망이라고? 뭐로부터 도망간단 말이야?"

아서는 어깨를 으쓱 올렸습니다. "그건 중요하지 않아요. 전 이제 안전해요. 그러니 제발 제가 돕게 해주세요."

"좋아, 하지만 기억해, 내가 널 주시하고 있다는 걸 말이야."

아서는 책 몇 권을 모으기 시작했습니다. 그것들은 모두 크기와 주제가 제각각이었습니다. 특히, 한 책이 그의 관심을 사로잡았습니다. 그것은 앞에 **개인적인 것**이라고 적혀 있었습니다.

도서관의 반대편 끝에서, 빙키, 머피, 그리고 프랜신은 팀을 이루어 찾고 있었습니다. 여자아이들은 책꽂이를 살펴보면서, 책상과 의자 위를 확인했습니다.

빙키는 네 발로 엎드려 있었습니다.

"이리 와, 작은 일기장아." 그가 말했다. "나오렴, 나와, 네가 어디에 있는지 간에."

프랜신은 그를 쳐다보았습니다. "넌 정말로 그게 도움이 된다고 생각하는 거야?"

page44

"해는 되지 않잖아." 빙키가 주장했습니다.

"일기장은 이렇게 찾기 힘들지 않아야 해." 머피가 말했습니다.

프랜신은 찡그렸습니다. "만약에 다른 사람이 그것을 먼저 찾지 않았다면 말이지."

머피가 헉 하고 숨을 쉬었습니다.

"무슨 일이야?" 빙키과 프랜신이 함께 물었습니다.

"아무것도 아니야." 머피가 말했습니다. "내가 막 생각을 했는데. 만약 일류 영화 제작자가 일기장을 찾았다면 어떻게 될까? 그녀는 아마 그것에 관한 영화를 만들고 싶을지도 몰라. 영화는 엄청난 성공을 거두겠지. 그 안에 나온 모든 사람이 온 세상에 알려질 거야. 그거 멋질 것 같지 않니?"

프랜신과 빙키는 서로를 바라보았습니다. "안 돼!" 그들이 소리쳤습니다.

"더 열심히 찾아." 프랜신이 말했습니다.

"훨씬 더 열심히." 빙키가 덧붙였습니다.

그들이 다시 찾기 시작했을 때 아서

가 다가왔습니다.

page 45

"머피, 너 혹시—"

"지금은 질문하지 마, 아서. 나 바쁜 거 안 보이니?"

사실, 아서는 왜 머피가 의자 방석 아래를 살펴보는지 궁금했습니다. 그는 그녀가 전에 그렇게 하는 것을 본 적이 없었습니다.

"난 그냥 네가 수 엘렌을 봤는지 알고 싶었어."

"한동안은 못 봤어,"

"너 혹시—?"

"내가 이걸 네게 일일이 다 풀어서 얘기해야 하겠어, 아서? 나는 **바—쁘—다—고**. 무슨 말인지 알겠니?"

"아주 분명히."

아서는 프랜신이 신문을 훑어보고 있는 곳으로 갔습니다.

"너는 어때, 프랜신?"

"내가 뭘?"

"넌 수 엘렌을 보았니?"

"아서, 지금 누가 어디에 있는지 다 파악하고 있지 않아. 난 할 일이 있다고."

page 46

"혹시 네가 그냥... 으악! 빙키, 너 뭐 하는 거야?"

빙키는 아서의 발 한쪽을 공중으로 들어 올렸습니다.

"그냥 확인하는 거야." 그가 말했습니다. 그는 아서의 발을 다시 내려놓았습니다.

"뭐, 내 발은 가만 둬. 그나저나, 너 수 엘렌을 못 봤지, 그렇지?"

"난 여기 아래에서는 아무도 볼 수 없어." 빙키가 인정했습니다.

아서는 그의 머리를 긁적였습니다. "그런데, 너 왜 그 아래에 있는 거야? 아니, 내게 알려주지 마. 난 가서 수 엘렌을 찾아야만 해."

"네가 지금 그녀를 찾는 것이 왜 그렇게 중요한 거야?" 머피가 물었습니다.

"아, 내가 그녀의 일기장을 찾았거든."

모두 얼어붙었습니다.

8장

page 47

아서, 머피, 빙키, 그리고 프랜신은 탁자에 둘러앉았습니다. 수 엘렌의 일기장이 가운데에 놓여 있었습니다. **개인적인 것**이라는 글자가 표지에서 그들을 노려보는 것 같았습니다.

빙키가 그것을 향해 손을 뻗었지만, 아서가 자신의 손을 표지 위에 올렸습니다.

"난 우리가 정말 이러면 안 된다고 생

각해." 그가 말했습니다. "내 말은, 넌 누가 네 일기장을 읽는 걸 원하겠니?"

"난 일기장을 갖고 있지 않아." 빙키가 말했습니다. "그러니 *내가* 어찌 알겠어?" 여전히, 그는 망설였습니다.

"솔직히, 아서." 프랜신이 말했습니다. "넌 그녀가 너에 대해 뭐라고 썼을지 궁금하지 않니?"

"뭐... 조금은... 그렇지."

"결정된 거야, 그럼." 머피가 말했습니다. "누가 먼저 읽을래?"

프랜신과 빙키는 서로를 쳐다보았습니다. "난 아니야." 그들이 함께 말했습니다.

"절대 나부터는 아니지." 아서가 말했습니다.

"뭐, 난 먼저 하고 싶진 않아." 머피가 말했습니다. "알았다... 우리는 일기장을 나침반처럼 돌리는 거야. 그게 멈췄을 때, 그 끝은 우리 가운데 한 사람을 가리킬 거야. 그 사람이 그것을 펼치면 되지."

"공정하게 들리네." 프랜신이 말했습니다.

"응." 빙키가 동의했습니다.

"아주." 아서가 말했습니다.

"그래서, 우리 돌릴까?" 머피가 물었습니다.

"**아니이이!**" 다른 모든 사람이 외쳤습니다.

"어쩌면 우리는 그냥 그것을 모서리로 세우는 거야." 프랜신이 말했습니다. "아마 그것이 떨어져서 펼쳐질 지도 몰라."

"그건 거의 우연 같을 거야." 머피가 말했습니다. "마음에 든다."

그들은 일기장을 똑바로 세웠습니다.

"그건 흔들거리는 것처럼 보여." 프랜신이 말했습니다.

"흔들거리는 건 좋지." 빙키가 동의했습니다.

일기장은 흔들리는 것처럼 보였을 지도 모르지만, 그것은 움직이지 않았습니다.

"어쩌면 우리는 충분히 열심히 쳐다보고 있지 않는지도 몰라." 머피가 말했습니다.

프랜신은 눈을 깜빡였습니다. "난 이보다 더 세게 쳐다볼 수는 없어. 난 사시가 되고 있다고."

"만약 강한 바람이 불어와서 일기장을 쓰러뜨려 펼친다면 어떨까?" 머피가 말했습니다.

"그래." 프랜신이 말했습니다. "그리고 그 바람이 책장을 넘길 수도 있지..."

그들은 바람이 불어오기를 인내심 있게 기다렸습니다. 그들은 기다리고 또 기다렸습니다.

"머피, 너 뭐 하는 거니?" 아서가 물었습니다.

머피는 얼굴이 빨개졌습니다. "나? 아무것도 아니야."

"봐! 너 또 그랬어." 아서는 그녀를 손가락으로 가리켰습니다. "너는 책에 입김을 불고 있잖아."

page 50

"바보처럼 그러지마." 머피가 말했습니다. "나는 그저, 음, 호흡 운동을 좀 하고 있는 것뿐이야."

빙키가 코웃음을 쳤습니다. "글쎄, 네가 어떤 결과라도 얻으려면 넌 훨씬 더 세게 숨을 쉬어야 할 거야."

그는 아주 깊은 숨을 내쉬었습니다.

"그건 또 뭐야?" 아서가 물었습니다.

"그냥 한숨이야, 아서." 프랜신이 말했습니다. "넌 한숨을 쉬었다고 빙키를 비난할 수 없어. 내 생각에 한숨을 좀 쉬는 게 내게 좀 도움이 될 것 같아."

아서는 자신의 팔짱을 꼈습니다. "이제 너희는 모두 씩씩거리고 있잖아. 이건 옳지 않아."

"난 아서에게 동의할 수밖에 없어." 빙키가 말했습니다. "난 바람으로는 충분할 것 같지 않아. 우리에게 필요한 건 지진이야."

"그럴 확률이 높진 않지." 아서가 말했습니다.

"누가 알겠어." 빙키가 말하면서, 탁자를 세게 발로 찼습니다.

책이 떨어졌지만—그것은 여전히 닫혀 있었습니다.

"이봐!" 아서가 말했습니다. "그건 반칙이야."

"그냥 실험해 본 거야." 빙키가 주장했습니다. "나는 지진이 도움이 되는지 확인해 보고 싶었다고."

page 52

"바람이랑 지진은 잊어버려." 프랜신이 말했습니다. "우리는 그냥 다 같이 그것을 읽어야만 하는지 몰라. 그렇게 한다면 우리는 모두 똑같이... 책임이 있는 거야."

누구도 그것에 반론을 제기할 수 없었습니다.

<h2 style="background-color:#2e9e5b;color:white;display:inline-block;padding:4px 12px">9장</h2>

page 53

"제 평생이 그 일기장 안에 있다고요!" 수 엘렌이 말했습니다.

"분명히 그렇겠지." 터너 선생님이 말했습니다. 그녀는 그녀를 위로하려고 수 엘렌을 직원 사무실로 데리고 갔습니다.

수 엘렌은 한숨 쉬었습니다. "그리고 이제 내 인생 전체가 사라져 버렸어요."

"저런, 저런, 얘야. 어쨌든, 너에게는 여전히 네 인생이 있어. 네 일기장에 관련해서는, 난 그게 나타날 거라고 확신한단다. 일기장들은 그냥 흔적도 없이 사라지지 않아."

"전 제가 여섯 살이었을 때부터 그 일기장을 갖고 있었어요. 전 1학년 첫 번째 날부터 그것을 쓰기 시작했다고요."

"그렇구나." 터너 선생님이 말했습니다.

"그때가 제가 학교에서 하루 종일 있던 첫 번째 날이었어요. 저는 전에는 학교에 그렇게 오래 있었던 적이 없었어요. 제가 집에 왔을 때, 엄마는 제가 그것에 대한 모든 것을 쓸 수 있도록 도와주셨어요."

page 54

터너 선생님이 고개를 끄덕였습니다.

"우리는 이야기 나누기 활동으로 수업을 시작했어요. 저는 가만히 앉아있는 게 힘들었어요. 그리고 저는 다른 여자 아이를 쳐다봤던 것이 기억나는데 왜냐하면 전 그렇게 옷을 차려 입은 사람을 본 적이 없었기 때문이었어요. 그리고는 선생님이 우리에게 이야기를 읽어주셨어요. '곰 세 마리 이야기'였던 것 같아요. 저는 골디락스에게 조심하라고 외쳤지만, 마지막에는 곰들을 안쓰럽게 생각했던 것을 기억해요. 적어도 전 제가 그랬던 것 같아요. 저는 확인해 봐야겠어요, 제—" 수 엘렌이 자신의 입술을 깨물었습니다. "하지만 저는 그것을 확인할 수 없잖아요, 그렇죠?"

터너 선생님이 일어나서 자신의 두 손을 비볐습니다. "있잖니, 여기 앉아 있는 대신에, 우리 계속 찾아보는 편이 더 좋을 것 같구나."

page 55

"만약에 다른 사람이 그것을 먼저 찾으면 어떡해요?"

터너 씨는 수 엘렌의 어깨를 토닥거렸습니다. "그러면 그들이 그것을 데스크로 가져 올 거고, 모두 괜찮아질 거야."

수 엘렌은 고개를 저었습니다. "하지만 그 사람이 그것을 돌려주기 전에 일기장을 읽어보면 어떡해요? 저 말고는 아무도 그것을 읽어본 적이 없어요."

"자, 수 엘렌, 내 생각엔 네가 없는 일을 갖고 속상해하는 것 같구나. 네가 모든 사람이 볼 수 있는 바로 그곳에 큰 글자로 **개인적인 것**이라고 써 놓았다고 네가 내게 말했잖니."

"맞아요." 수 엘렌이 인정했습니다.

"아니, 그렇다면, 넌 아무것도 걱정할 게 없네."

"수 엘렌!"

아서와 다른 아이들이 그녀를 향해 다가오고 있었습니다.

page 57

"우리는 너에게 줄 것이 있어." 아서가 말했습니다. 그는 일기장을 내밀었습니다.

수 엘렌은 헉 하고 숨을 내쉬었습니다. "너 그걸 어디서 찾았어?" 그녀는 일기장을 받아 들었고 그것을 가슴에 끌어안았습니다.

"수레들 중 하나 위에서," 아서가 말했습니다. "나는 이걸 바로 너에게 돌려주려고 했는데—"

"하지만 우리가 그를 막았어." 머피가 말했습니다.

"왜냐하면 우리는 안을 살펴보고 싶었기 때문이야." 프랜신이 덧붙였습니다.

"그랬다고?" 수 엘렌이 일기장을 더 세게 끌어안았습니다. "하지만 이건 **개인적인 것**이야. 여기 바로 표지 위에 그렇게 쓰여 있잖아."

"걱정하지 마." 아서가 말했습니다. "우리는 보지 않았어."

"비록 우리가 바람과 지진 때문에 유혹을 받긴 했지만." 빙키가 말했습니다.

수 엘렌은 이해할 수 없었지만, 어쨌든 그녀는 미소 지었습니다. "글쎄, 이유야 어찌 되었건, 고마워. 그리고 비록 내가 내 규칙들 가운데 하나를 어기게 되겠지만, 난 오늘 밤에 내가 무엇에 대해 쓸지 너희에게 말해줄 수 있어."

"그게 뭔데?" 빙키가 물었습니다.

page 58

수 엘렌은 미소 지었습니다. "바로 내가 세상에서 가장 좋은 친구들을 두었

다는 것이지."

10장

page 59

수 엘렌이 도서관을 떠나려고 할 때, 빙키가 그녀를 위해 문을 열어 주었습니다.

"내가 해 줄게." 그가 말했습니다.

수 엘렌은 놀란 것처럼 보였습니다. "어머, 빙키, 난 네가 이렇게 신사인 줄은 몰랐네."

"난 그렇지 않아! 그러니까, 글쎄, 보통 때는 안 그래." 그는 땅을 바라보았습니다. "그리고 네가 다른 사람에게 말한다면, 난 부인할 거야."

수 엘렌이 미소 지었습니다. "걱정하지 마. 네 비밀은 내가 지켜 줄게."

그녀는 자전거 보관대로 계속 갔고, 그곳에서는 머피가 출발할 준비를 하고 있었습니다.

page 60

"또 보자, 수 엘렌." 머피가 페달 위에 자기 발을 올려 놓더니—멈추었습니다. "그나저나, 네가 이야기에 쓸 생각이 필요하다면 난 오늘밤에 집에 있을 거야."

"이야기라니?"

"있잖아, 아름답고, 부유하고, 또 지략이 있는 공주가 세상을 구하는 이야

기 말이야.”

“오. 고마워, 머피. 만약 그런 게 떠오르면, 내가 전화할게.”

머피는 고개를 끄덕였고 자전거를 타고 갔습니다.

“오, 수 엘렌.” 프랜신이 말하면서, 그녀의 뒤로 달려왔습니다. “네가 네 자전거 자물쇠를 푸는 동안 내가 네 책을 들어줄게. 네가 다치는 걸 원하지 않으니까!”

“음, 고마워.”

“내가 또 너를 도와줄 것은 없을까? 알다시피, 난 정말 친절하잖니. 그리고 또한, 배려심이 깊기도 하고. 그리고 내가 *착하다*고 이야기했나? 착한 것은 내 가장 좋은 장점이야.”

수 엘렌은 혼란스러운 얼굴이었습니다.

“뭐, 내일 보자.” 프랜신이 말했습니다. “숙제 하는 데에 문제가 있거나 그냥 이야기를 하고 싶으면 전화해줘. 그리고 즐겁게 글 쓰렴!”

수 엘렌은 고개를 저으면서 자신의 자전거 헬멧을 썼습니다. 그녀는 일기를 쓰는 것이 그녀를 이렇게 인기 있게 하리라고 전혀 예상하지 못했습니다.

그녀가 이에 대해 여전히 생각하는 동안 아서가 도서관 밖으로 나왔습니다.

“아서, 아무도 내 일기장을 읽지 않았다고 확신하니?” 그녀가 물었습니다.

“걱정하지 마, 수 엘렌. 그건 여전히 개인적인 거니까.” 그가 말을 멈추었습니다. “나한테 묻고 싶은 게 또 있니? 아니면 나에게 말해줄 거라도?”

“없는 것 같은데.”

“있잖아, 난 비판을 정말 잘 받아들여. 그리고 난 늘 더 내 자신을 발전시킬 준비가 되어있지. 그러니까 말하는 걸 망설이지 마.”

수 엘렌은 자신의 자전거 위에 올라탔습니다. “그러지 않을게. 너 정말 일기장에 대해서 확실한 거지….”

“확실해.”

“좋아. 넌 좀 당황했을지도 몰라.”

“내가?” 아서가 눈을 깜박였습니다. “내가 개선해야 할 수 있는 많은 방법에 대해 네가 써놓았을 거라고 난 생각해.”

수 엘렌은 어리둥절해 보였습니다. “아니야. 사실은, 나는 너에 관해서 꽤 좋은 말들을 썼어.”

아서는 얼굴을 붉혔습니다. “정말? 어떤 것들 말이야?”

“미안. 난 말할 수 없어.”

아서는 인상을 찌푸렸습니다. “그건 불공평해!”

“다음에 보자!” 수 엘렌이 자전거를 타고 떠나면서, 말했습니다.

“좋아.” 아서가 그녀를 향해 외쳤습니다. “그렇다면, 난 나만의 일기장을 쓰기 시작하겠어.”

수 엘렌이 끽 하는 소리를 내며 멈췄습니다.

“네가 그런다고? 넌 그 안에 뭐라고 쓸 건데?”

아서는 미소 지었습니다. “그건 말이야.” 그가 말했습니다. “내 작은 비밀이야.”

Chapter 1

1. D At one table, Sue Ellen was sitting alone. She didn't look up when anyone walked by, nor did she pay any attention to passing conversations. She was concentrating on writing in her diary.

2. B Sue Ellen put down her pen. That was enough for now. She loved having a diary, a special place to write down her private thoughts. It wasn't that her ideas were always great or important. But she liked putting the words on paper, where she could look at them.

3. A She closed the diary and traced the edge of the binding with her finger. Sue Ellen had designed the cover herself. My Diary, she had printed neatly with a sparkle pen. Underneath, she had added PRIVATE and DO NOT OPEN in large letters.

4. C The library clock struck four times, reminding Sue Ellen that it was time to go. She picked up all the books she wanted to check out and piled them on her The library clock struck four times, reminding Sue Ellen that it was time to go. She picked up all the books she wanted to check out and piled them on her

5. A Ms. Turner began checking out the books, Sue Ellen spread them on the counter. When she got to the last one, she expected to see her diary underneath. But all she saw was her notebook. Immediately, she searched among the other books.

Chapter 2

1. C Sue Ellen dragged herself back to the checkout counter. Her face was red, and her eyes watery. "What's wrong?" asked Ms. Turner, who could see that Sue Ellen was upset.

2. B "That's very specific," said Ms. Turner. "It should make our search easier. Don't worry—we'll find it. I'll tell everyone on the staff to be on the lookout."

3. B Sue Ellen paused because she heard some laughing. It was exactly the kind of sound a girl might make if she was looking at a secret diary. "I'll be back," she told Ms. Turner. Sue Ellen traced the sound to the comer, where

Francine was hunched over some pages.

4. A "Of course not," said Francine. "It's a joke book. What would I be doing with your diary?"

5. D "I've never had a diary," said Francine. "What do you write in it?" "My ideas, what's happened during the day. Private thoughts. It's very important that I find it, Francine. I mean, there's stuff in there about everyone." Francine's eyes opened wide. "Everyone? When you say *everyone*, you mean *everyone*?" "Yes, yes, but that's not what matters now." "It matters to me," said Francine. "What have you been writing?"

Chapter 3

1. A "Hmmm," said Muffy. "Maybe she wrote something about you—something she doesn't want you to read." "About me?" Francine put her hands on her hips. "But what would she write about me?" "Maybe all the mean things you've done to her."

2. C Francine looked surprised. "What things?" Muffy folded her arms. "Like pushing her in the mud yesterday."

3. D "Well, you laughed." "Of course, I laughed. It was funny. She was covered with mud."

4. C *"Ah! And what is the nature of this emergency? Sue Ellen held out her arms. "Can't you tell? Francine just pushed me in the mud." The doctor stroked his beard. "So I see," he said.*

5. A *"Ah, yes," he said. "Pushing. Laughing. Eating the fruit filling in your snack pie and leaving you only the crust." He sighed. "I'm afraid your friend exhibits all the signs of acute ogre-ism." "Ogre-ism?"*

Chapter 4

1. A "Francine is so excitable sometimes," Muffy said to herself. "Sue Ellen probably didn't write about her at all." She paused, leaning against a shelf. "Of course, she did have to write about something. Everyday events can be so boring, though. She probably has to make up stories . . ."

2. C Muffy saw herself looking into a long mirror. She was dressed as a princess, in a long flowing dress with a jeweled crown on her head.

3. B *"Help us!" shouted the villagers. "Help us, rich and beautiful and smart Princess Millicenta!"*

4. B *She started clanking down the tower stairs, but after a few moments, the clanking stopped. "What's the matter" asked Muffy. "Why have you stopped?" "Ooof," Sue Ellen called up. "I'm stuck in the doorway." She gasped. "And the dragon is approaching!"*

5. C *As the dragon prepared to toast Sue Ellen to a crisp, Muffy spritzed it with a bottle of her perfume. The dragon's fire was snuffed out.*

Chapter 5

1. B Binky just shrugged. "Okay, okay. But whatever you are, you're blocking the shelf. I need to look for a book back there."

2. D "I saw a book like that," said Binky. "It was on the floor. I put it on one of the carts."

3. C Binky was impressed. "Everybody, huh?" he said to himself. Keeping a diary sounded like a lot of work. Writing one didn't appeal to him. But if Sue Ellen was writing about everybody . . .

4. C Dear Diary: Today was very special. I was able to spend almost all my time with Binky Banes, the man of my dreams.

5. A I can tell that the other boys all look up to Binky. Who can blame them? I only wish I could get Binky to notice me. I try smiling at him a lot, but he only asks me what's wrong with my face. I follow him around on the playground, but he wants to know if I'm lost or something. I've even started bringing him extra desserts for lunch. At least that gets his attention. And I know he always burps afterward.

Chapter 6

1. D "What's the matter, Binky?" said Arthur. "You look like the Statue of Liberty." "Huh?" Binky dropped his arm like a stone.

2. B "Um, never mind." Binky wanted to change the subject. "Did you hear? Sue Ellen lost her diary. I put it on the cart." Arthur frowned. "Why didn't you give it back to her?" "I didn't know it was her diary then. It was just some book with PRIVATE written across the front."

3. D *Sue Ellen looked at the titles.* "Mystery of the Mummy's Curse, Eerie Canals of Mars. *Arthur, I can't believe you read this stuff." "Why not?" "It's not good for you. Don't you get nightmares?"*

4. C *Sue Ellen nodded. "You're not perfect, Arthur. In fact, you're wide open for improvement I've kept track of your flaws in my diary."*

5. A *Sue Ellen moved along the paper. "'Number 78: Doesn't take criticism well.' Now, are you going to sit still? We've got work to do."*

Chapter 7

1. A The assistant jumped back. "How do I know you won't try to tackle me again?" "I wasn't tackling you," said Arthur. "I was just trying to escape."

2. B Arthur began gathering some of the books. They came in all different sizes and subjects. One, in particular, caught his attention. It said PRIVATE on the front.

3. D At the other end of the library, Binky, Muffy, and Francine were hunting as a team. The girls were looking through the bookcases, checking on the desks and chairs. Binky was down on his hands and knees.

4. A "No questions now, Arthur. Can't you see I'm busy?" Actually, Arthur had wondered why Muffy was looking under the seat cushions. He had never seen her do that before. "I just wanted to know if you've seen Sue Ellen." "Not for a while." "Can you—?" "Do I need to spell it out for you, Arthur? I'm *B-U-S-Y.* Get the message?"

5. B Arthur scratched his head. "Why are you down there, anyway? Wait, don't tell me. I have to go find Sue Ellen." "What's so important that you have to find her now?" Muffy asked. "Oh, I found her diary."

Chapter 8

1. C "I really don't think we should do this," he said. "I mean, would you want someone to read *your* diary?" "I don't *have* a diary," said Binky, " so how would *I* know?" Still, he hesitated.

2. B "Well, I don't want to be first," said Muffy. "I know . . . We could spin the diary around like a compass. When it stopped, the top would point to one of us. That person would have to open it."

3. A "Maybe we could just stand it on end," said Francine. "Maybe it would fall over and open." "That would almost be an accident," said Muffy. "I like it."

4. C "There! You did it again." Arthur pointed a finger at her. "You're blowing at the book." "Don't be silly," said Muffy. "I'm just, um, doing some breathing exercises." Binky snorted. "Well, you're going to have to breathe a lot harder if you want to get anywhere." He let out a very deep breath.

5. D "Forget the wind and the earthquake," said Francine. "Maybe we should just all read it together. That way we'll all be equally . . . guilty."

Chapter 9

1. A "I've had that diary ever since I was six. I started it on the first day of first grade."

2. B "What if someone else finds it first?" Ms. Turner patted Sue Ellen on the shoulder. "Then they'll turn it in at the desk, and all will be well."

3. B "Now, Sue Ellen, I think you're getting yourself upset over nothing. You told me it says PRIVATE in big letters right where everyone can see it." "That's true," Sue Ellen admitted. "Why, then, you have nothing to worry about."

4. C "On one of the carts," said Arthur. "I was going to give it right back to you—" "But we stopped him." said Muffy. "Because we wanted to look inside," Francine added. "You did?" Sue Ellen hugged the diary tighter. "But it's PRIVATE. It says so right on the cover." "Don't worry," said Arthur. "We didn't look."

5. D "What's that?" asked Binky. Sue Ellen smiled. "That I have the best friends in the world."

Chapter 10

1. B As Sue Ellen was leaving the library, Binky held open the door for her. "Allow me," he said. Sue Ellen looked surprised. "Why, Binky, I didn't know you were such a gentleman."

2. C "By the way, I'll be home tonight if you need any ideas for stories." "Stories?"

3. A "Is there anything else I can help you with? I'm very friendly, you know. And considerate, too. And have I mentioned nice? Being nice is my best thing."

4. C "That's good. You might have been embarrassed." "Me?" Arthur blinked. "I suppose you've written down a lot of ways I could improve." Sue Ellen looked puzzled. "No. Actually, I said some pretty nice things about you."

5. B "Sorry. My lips are sealed." Arthur frowned. "That's not fair!" "See you later!" said Sue Ellen, riding off. "All right," Arthur called after her. "In that case, I'm going to start a diary of my own." Sue Ellen screeched to a stop. "You are? What are you going to put in it?" Arthur smiled. "That," he said, "will be my little secret."

아서와 사라진 일기장
(Arthur and the Lost Diary)

1판 1쇄   2016년 1월 4일
1판 7쇄   2020년 8월 7일

지은이   Marc Brown
기획   이수영
책임편집   김보경 정소이
콘텐츠제작및감수   롱테일북스 편집부
저작권   김보경
마케팅   김보미 정경훈

펴낸이   이수영
펴낸곳   (주)롱테일북스
출판등록   제2015-000191호
주소   04043 서울특별시 마포구 양화로 12길 16-9(서교동) 북앤빌딩 3층
전자메일   helper@longtailbooks.co.kr
(학원 · 학교에서 본도서를 교재로 사용하길 원하시는 경우 전자메일로 문의주시면
자세한 안내를 받으실 수 있습니다.)

ISBN   979-11-86701-05-8   14740

롱테일북스는 (주)북하우스 퍼블리셔스의 계열사입니다.

이 도서의 국립중앙도서관 출판시도서목록(CIP)은 서지정보유통지원시스템 홈페이지(http://seoji.nl.go.kr)와
국가자료공동목록시스템(http://www.nl.go.kr/kolisnet)에서 이용하실 수 있습니다. (CIP 제어번호 : CIP2015033029)